the **brightwork**
companion

the brightwork companion

tried-and-true methods
and **strongly held opinions**
in thirteen and one-half chapters

REBECCA J. WITTMAN

AUTHOR OF **BRIGHTWORK: THE ART OF FINISHING WOOD**

INTERNATIONAL MARINE / McGRAW-HILL

CAMDEN, MAINE ▪ NEW YORK ▪ CHICAGO ▪ SAN FRANCISCO ▪ LISBON ▪ LONDON ▪ MADRID ▪ MEXICO CITY ▪ MILAN ▪ NEW DELHI ▪ SAN JUAN ▪ SEOUL ▪ SINGAPORE ▪ SYDNEY ▪ TORONTO

The McGraw·Hill Companies

5 6 7 8 9 10 KHL KHL 14 13 12

Library of Congress Cataloging-in-Publication Data
Wittman, Rebecca J.
   The brightwork companion : tried-and-true methods and strongly held opinions in thirteen and one-half chapters / Rebecca J. Wittman.— 1st ed.
       p.   cm.
Includes bibliographical references and index.
  ISBN 0-07-142277-3 (pbk.)
  1. Wooden boats—Maintenance and repair. 2. Wood finishing. I. Title.
VM322.W58 2004
623.8´207—dc22   2003018145

Questions regarding the content of this book should be
    addressed to
International Marine
P.O. Box 220
Camden, ME 04843
www.internationalmarine.com

Questions regarding the ordering of this book should be
    addressed to
The McGraw-Hill Companies
Customer Service Department
P.O. Box 547
Blacklick, OH 43004
Retail customers: 1-800-262-4729
Bookstores: 1-800-722-4726

for my Garth . . .

        and our David

contents

part three: *tools, materials,*
and resources

preface

In 1990, when International Marine released *Brightwork: The Art of Finishing Wood,* the overwhelming response took both publisher and author by surprise. Thirteen years later, *Brightwork* is still selling strongly, still finding new fans, and we're still amazed and gratified.

At first blush, this *Brightwork Companion* may seem a shameless ripoff of its predecessor.

A shameless STRIP-off would be more like it. In the words of one book distributor, "It's *Brightwork* without the romance" (though there *is* a bit of bodice-ripping prose in chapter 2).

Brightwork is often accused of being the varnishing bible. Why would it need a companion, you ask? I'll tell you why: all that fretting about the need to purchase *two* of those $35 best-sellers became too much. "I need one to mess up at the boat; I need another one to display on the coffee table!" It was too much for my latent Catholic sensibilities (the blasphemy, the guilt!). Too much for the publishers—decent, unassuming people who hadn't realized that this dilemma accounted for so many books sold. Together, burdened, we resolved to find relief for our collective shame. And so, here it is. Half the price (sort of)—zero guilt . . . a *Brightwork Cliff Notes for Dummies.* In cookbook form.

Apologies for either book, of course, could only be tongue in cheek. Both the publishers and I are very proud of the contribution *Brightwork* has made in the yacht refinishing community since its first release. It has helped identify solidarity among thousands of artisans who have long toiled in private, who appreciated finding printed validation of their own finishing passions and tentatively held theories. This new book does not replace but functions as a utilitarian adjunct to its predecessor. *Brightwork* is Mel Gibson. The *Companion* is the stunt double. The little guy steps in when it's time for the dirty work, prostrating itself to the noble cause, while the big star sits on the coffee table and garners all the glory. It does leave out much of the earlier romance. More curious artisans, not yet in possession of the first book, might want to reach deeper into their wallet for things like the evolution of bright finishes, the "Yacht Refinishing Commandments," the tenets of Dockside Etiquette, tales of petulant violinists, and the complete etymology of that enchanting appellation "Varnish." But they wouldn't have to. If they just want to get the finishing process going, this "Companion" blazes a shorter path to the starting gate, without eliminating anything essential to the process.

The Brightwork Companion brings the actual labors described in the earlier text into clipped instruction and Germanic form. It is a working distillation of the first book: checklists and bullets and an easier-to-follow, "do this, then this, then this" drill. Marching orders, really, with still a few little entertainments along the way. Use this book the way you would a cookbook. Be seduced by the pictures, read through the recipes, and get excited. Highlight the lists, buy the materials, then prop up the book and get to work.

And never fret about spilling sticky stuff on the pages. Those splatters are testimony to work that has been done energetically and with artistic abandon. When all your labors are behind you, you can always slide *Brightwork* off the coffee table, still glossy and clean, and settle in with larger, more glamorous tales of romance and intrigue.

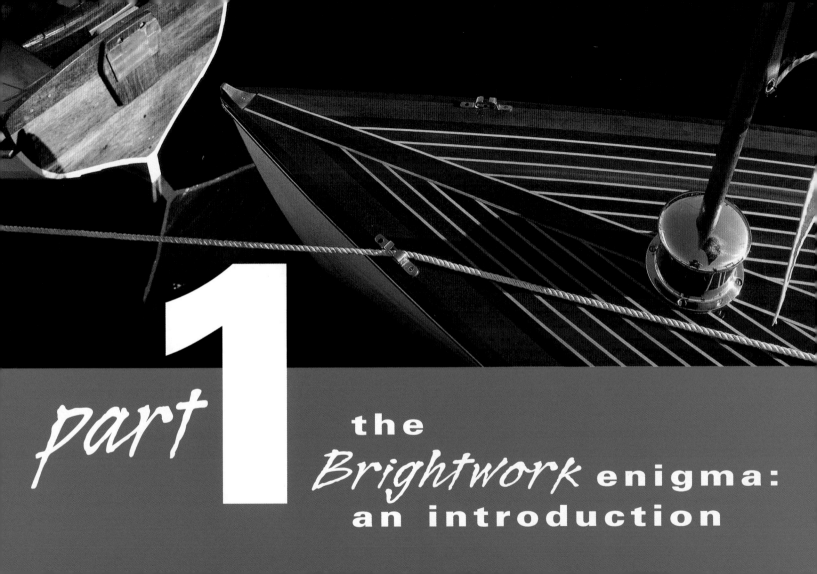

part **1**

the
Brightwork enigma:
an introduction

1

chapter

the more things change, the more they stay the same . . .

"All there is in varnishing is the putting of it on surfaces with a brush." —F. Maire

My family and I are suckers for a garage sale. We consider such events akin to an archaeological dig. For years, we've slaked our thirst for kitsch and sated our hunger for cultural enlightenment (OK, so we've been out searching for bargains like everybody else . . .) on weekend expeditions through other people's junk. One lazy Saturday morning on such an excursion, I found myself spelunking through the tightly crammed basement of a recently deceased member of the painting trades. The dear departed, who according to his not very emotive wife had "spent forty-five years up a ladder," had been something of a pack rat. Among his now devalued treasures—buried in old, musty tarps between stacks of antediluvian issues of *Popular Mechanics*—languished a paint-spattered copy of what must have been the bible of the coatings trade back at the turn of the 20th century. Gold-leafed lettering regally proclaimed the title:

Modern Painter's Cyclopedia

I'd just blown my budget for the day, a crumpled $10 bill, on a perfect twenty-five-foot telescoping ladder (the painter's ghost doubtless haunting its rungs) and was trying to escape the property before my larceny was realized. But suddenly, the partially hidden title of this old book came into focus and screamed out to me. The word *Modern*, adorning something so clearly antique, hinted at the possibility of entertainment. I paused.

The Modern Painter's Cyclopedia *is not merely the compiling and putting together the stale writings and antiquated methods which have been put to use by many persons to make up a book to sell, but has been completely rewritten and the subject matter handled in such a way as to describe the latest methods used in performing the work.*

"How much?" I asked. The painter's widow sensed my thrill and, likely wising up to her earlier miscalculation on the ladder, demanded no less than one dollar. I countered with a brazen fifty

Old paint on canvas, as it ages, sometimes becomes transparent. When that happens it is possible, in some pictures, to see the original lines: a tree will show through a woman's dress, a child makes way for a dog, a large boat is no longer on an open sea. That is called pentimento because the painter "repented," changed his mind. Perhaps it would be well to say that the old conception, replaced by a later choice, is a way of seeing and then seeing again.

—Lillian Hellman

In brightwork, too, the layers of our refinishing efforts can also be peeled back like skins of an onion to betray our degree of commitment, or lack thereof.

cents. But she knew she had me and stood her price. I bummed a buck from my son and fled with the book and butterflies in my stomach, tingling at the possibility of having unearthed a bona fide treasure.

One of the greatest drawbacks to the beginner in his attempts at applying varnish is his fear that he is putting on too much and that it will sag. Therefore, he works and works it out to the last limit; he does what is known as "skinning it on" in varnish slang. Now, skinned on varnish never looks well and makes the job look like a man in a dress suit with plow shoes on. Varnish, to look well, must be put on full.

I, the wimp who never reads in cars, finally pulled my nose out of the book's ivoried pages when we were halfway home, and then only because a cloud of carsickness had begun to settle over me. When we arrived, the ladder remained tied atop the car and life swirled about and without me as I remained in my seat, entranced, unstringing pearls of ancient finishing wisdom.

He will probably know as much about it if told to dip his brush in the varnish pot and rub it on the surface where it is wanted as he would in a long essay which he will get mixed up in, and which will puzzle him much more than it will enlighten him.

My sentiments exactly! In fact, echoing through many of the pages were *countless* paraphrasings of my own sentiments, so many that elation and carsickness eventually gave way to a cloud of déjà vu. The author of this book, the mysterious F. Maire, had seemingly appropriated techniques, advice, and philosophies that I *myself* had published in so many words in 1990, in *Brightwork.* But how was this possible? My book had come into print ninety-some years after his. (Or hers?) I realize the implications here would logically indict *me*, but this volume did not come into my hands until my book was enjoying its fourth printing. I had written mine, at least the chapters that chanted methodology, from personal experience. With my own two hands I had varnished and prepped and developed the body of knowledge limned in those pages. Was this author prescient of my ten years at the mast? Had I somehow, unwittingly, been a time-traveling thief?

Neither, of course, is the answer. We had both developed our finishing gospel by dipping into a community well of varnishing wisdom, a wisdom that has been flowing cosmically through the ages, stopping at F. Maire's brush on its way to mine, as it now flows through mine on its way to yours.

Varnish, once taken out of the can and exposed to the air should never be poured back into the can. How many have learned this lesson only after bitter experiences! They will argue that it is foolish and that no possible harm can follow—and they learn after it is too late that it ruins a good varnish to pour it back into the can, and that it queers all the rest of it in the can.

The fact is that, like the original formulation of varnish—which through two thousand years has not truly changed—the technique and rhythm of varnish application, too, remains a constant. In researching my original book, my heart quickened at each new bend in the evolutionary path of this noble coating. I was knocked out by the fact that the same ingredients used by the ancient Egyptians—oils and resins—still underpin in essence the standard formulations for spar varnish, the old, reliable finish that people keep coming back to after all the "modern" cans on the shelf disappoint.

If the varnisher will bear in mind that the varnish manufacturer who knows all the particulars and the peculiarities of every one of his tanks should certainly be the proper one to make the mixing, and that if he has failed to make it good, certainly the man who knows nothing whatever about that varnish or what he mixes with it, will certainly make a mess, and probably a botch of it.

In preparing this new variation on the theme of *Brightwork*, my heart now leaps at the fact that essentially ancient techniques still make up the modus operandi that has been handed down, unchanged, from each "modern" varnisher plying the trade at the turn of every century since varnish was first invented. It is a legacy that anchors a fading but tenacious art, a transfer made complete through that mysterious process of transgenerational osmosis. It is the same magic that infuses in me the sewing prowess of my grandmother, without my ever so much as having had a needle-threading lesson from her.

It is almost needless to have to warn against varnishing a job where it will be subjected to dust, changes of temperature and the thousand and one other causes which will make varnishes go wrong. Only those who are familiar with the host of "make-varnish-go-wrong-agencies" have any idea of their multitude and extent. It also seems as needless to say that it requires skill and experience.

The Brightwork Companion, while a faithful distillation of *Brightwork: The Art of Finishing Wood*, is also a slight updating, a making "modern" of my own earlier text. In certain areas of this age-old art, there are bound to be developments within our lifetimes that improve our lives—indeed that can extend them—as finishers. I have yet to be convinced that these developments need involve the varnish formula itself. But certain products—methylene chloride stripping compounds, for example—are such despicable agents that they, by their very existence, mandate replacement. I held my nose (literally and figuratively) when instructing fellow finishers and readers of the original volume on the use of those products, wishing there were a less personally hazardous but equally effective formula to employ when chemical stripping was the only choice. Happily, now there is, and the replacement almost single-handedly warrants revision of the book. Tools, too, rightfully enjoy an evolution toward user-friendliness and more efficient expenditure of one's precious time. I've added a couple sanders to my tool bag since the first book came out, ones that don't replace my Speed-Bloc but augment it for surface refinements that heretofore required precious elbow grease and willing hands. At the same time, there are passages to report: the loss of certain beloved tools, victims of the corporate bottom line that forces us to take care of and treasure what we have and, as those old standbys break down, open our minds to lesser surrogates.

And so, within this new, handier configuration of *Brightwork*, there is worthy impetus for revision. But it is still the timelessness of varnishing itself that warrants commitment of ink to paper. The reminder that we are carrying on an ancient art is never redundant. I write this new book to make it easier for my fellow artisans, at a time in human history when nobody seems to have time to slow down and do things that require patience, to do this divine thing, patiently and lovingly and joyfully, and as efficiently as possible without sacrificing what makes it divine.

It may remain one of the many other mysteries connected with varnish which no amount of reasoning can explain satisfactorily to one seeking to understand it. Varnish is a touchy affair—worse than an old maid to handle. It will only be handled in its own good way and no other.

My $1 garage sale treasure, a little volume of modernity now almost a hundred years old, reinforces in me the greatest varnishing truth, something I've always believed but adore finding validated in print: that the things that are vital and honorable about varnishing are the parts we do with our hearts, our hands, and that portion of our brain that houses common sense. These are what never change, the things that will prevail. In spite of the influence of slothful practitioners and "Profit-Über-Alles" coatings and equipment manufacturers, and despite the prognostications of the plastics-everywhere set, there will still be a generation of varnishers a hundred years from now, artisans who cherish not just what flows from the brush, but dear souls who cannot help but spend "forty-five years up the ladder." May that cosmic flow never ebb.

Some men are born good varnishers and fall into the right way of it like a gosling to a pond of water, and no one knows till they try what they may be capable of. With care, the proper use of the brush can be acquired, when it is not natural to a person. It is, of course, much more pleasant to have been born a varnisher, but some of the best varnishers commenced by aggravated cases of sagging in their first attempts at it. "Try, try again," is a good motto, if it is old fashioned. The man who is observant will note where he has erred and the next job will be more perfect because the experience had on the former one will guard him against committing the same mistake again; such men will grow into good varnishers.

—F. Maire

2 afflictions

and cures . . .

everybody knows the one about the two happiest days in a boatowner's life . . .

Discovering that special boat down at the dealer's dock, resplendent in all her gleaming varnish and satiny oil finish, is like being introduced to the most beautiful woman at the party. Your heart quickens, you size her up from the closest possible range, you dare to touch her once, and then you want to know her better so you start asking questions. You make a date for a day of sailing together. When you get out alone with her, your initial feelings are confirmed; you find her company invigorating, you're intoxicated by her countenance. You dream about her day and night, until finally you can't stand it another minute. You tender the proposal. Legal documents are signed.

You get her home, you spend passionate hours together, and then you decide it's time to see what she can really do for you, so you start putting her through her paces. You ask her to impress your friends and the boss and the boss's wife. You ask her to be your port in the storm, to be there when you need her, but not to be a burden on you when you've got more important things on your mind. Life crowds in, and pretty soon the bloom begins to fade. You're busy: long workdays, the golf tournament, season tickets at the ballpark. She's looking neglected; she starts seeming a little dark and sad. You know you should spend more time with her, but you're being pulled from the other side. Before you know it, she's asking you to take her on a trip, hinting at that block of time you'd hoped to reserve for the pilgrimage to St. Andrews with the guys. You feel guilty, but the old ties are strong. You tell yourself, "She knows she's loved."

Then one day you discover she's a total mess. The gleam in your eye becomes a tear of remorse. You haven't the slightest recollection what you were thinking when you fell in love . . .

"What happened?" you ask yourself.

The seductive finish people first encounter on a boat is not some glistening manifestation of the siren's song. That gorgeous varnish, the thing that renders a floating vessel rapturous and makes your heart skip a beat, is a precious asset and tangible proof of its steward's *devoted attention*. On your boat, it is sweet testament to the maintenance program you set up from the day you first declared, "I want her to be mine." To paraphrase Fanny Brice, your brightwork is the "beautiful reflection" of her love's affection . . .

In charting a maintenance course, there are two simple passageways to brightwork bliss:

OPTION A: you do the finishing yourself

For those choosing Option A (and these are the majority of boatowners), the instructions found in the pages of this book should, I hope, mitigate any challenges. But first, I submit a little quiz to ensure your stewardship appropriately falls under that column:

1. Do you have time to do your own finishing?
For the uninitiated, apply Murphy's Law of Estimating: Take your best guess, double it, and then add 10 percent . . .

2. Do you *like* to do your own finishing?
In other words, do you head off to the boat—sandpaper in hand—whistling or cursing?

3. Is your marriage on solid ground?
Does your spouse see your passion for varnishing as a threat or, worse, a welcome respite from your presence?

If you gave three "No" answers to the quiz, and your boat sports a vast acreage of brightwork, I might recommend hiring the work out while you go on a second honeymoon.

OPTION B: you wave your magic checkbook over the finish

For those inclined toward Option B—for whatever reason—the information you find in this book should help you comprehend the tremendous labors entailed in finishing work and, accordingly, why it costs what it costs.

option A: *you do the finishing yourself*

CHOOSING THE FINISH

There are countless variations on the varnish and oil themes, and an ideal "finish program" can be formulated only when one understands not just what is *in* the can, but how the contents of that can relate to the wood being finished.

- **Varnish** brings out the beauty in wood and is the strongest protector of all the bright finishes. Beauty arrives by the third coat, but protection does not come into play until after the eighth. Eight to ten coats of varnish provide the best finish foundation for follow-up varnish management.

- **A true oil finish** also brings out the beauty in wood but affords exterior wood little if not completely transient protection. Oil finishes require the same amount of prep labor as varnish, then disappear in a matter of months without constant (read: monthly!) refresher coats. I have another name for "oil finish" on exteriors. It is "full-time job."

- **A "sealer"** is not a finish. It is a thin, solvent-intense formula meant *only* to deliver a "seal" to the deepest reaches of the wood's grain, in preparation for a subsequent application of an oil or varnish. That seal will last fully intact about a week when exposed to the weather.

- **Bare wood** is the "no-finish" finish option. It looks easy, but it demands initial prep similar to that given wood slated for a finish: properly bleached and sanded, and faithful, appropriate cleaning to forestall mildew. The decision to leave wood bare first requires that it be a wood that can survive without a finish. Teak, with its natural storehouse of oils, is an ideal "bare wood." So is ironwood. Mahogany fares best—and shows off its most beautiful self—with varnish protection. Veneer of any kind should *never* be left bare.

Bottom line . . . for interiors, varnish and oil are both options.

But for EXTERIOR woods, the only SMART finish is . . . VARNISH!

Once in a while, despite your best intentions, the finish gets away from you. When that happens, it doesn't signal the end of the relationship. It just means it's time to turn your attentions fully in the direction of your erstwhile seductress . . .

THE AFFLICTION	THE CURE
Slightly dulled gloss but generally unbroken varnish skin.	Refresh all brightwork with two coats varnish.
Moderately dull surface but still no breaks.	Refresh all brightwork with two coats varnish.
Dull surface, splitting of finish at joints but solid otherwise.	Mend joints, refresh all brightwork with two coats varnish.
Dull surface, split varnish at joints, some lifting along edges.	Scratch and patch all joints and lifted areas, then refresh all brightwork with two or three coats varnish.
Checking or eroding of varnish surfaces, split and lifting finish at joints with discoloration of wood beneath.	Scratch and patch all lifted varnish areas (pages 102–3), bleaching discolored wood and giving the wood plenty of time to air out before sealing. Determine and fix causes of major problems. Refresh all brightwork with at least three coats.
"Varnish starvation"—wholesale erosion of finish, split and lifted finish at all joints and edges; weathered or blackened bare wood in places where finish has worn away.	If more than half the brightwork is in this condition, strip everything and refinish from clean, bare wood.
Finish has been patched and recoated faithfully for more than six years but still looks ratty and lifeless after each refresher.	Take it all off and bring in the new guard. And pat yourself on the back for being such a dedicated steward.

. . . and where do I find guidance in effecting those cures?

The answers to all your prayers can be found with careful perusal of chapters 9 and 10.

cause & effect . . .

Aside from simple neglect, there is often a specific culprit (poor drainage, for example) that, unless identified and fixed, can recurrently degrade a finish and, in some cases, ultimately ruin the wood itself. Anytime you encounter a dramatic finish problem, try to determine the greater underlying cause of decline, and make the repair before you address the refinishing.

an ounce of prevention . . .

Seventy-five percent of the challenge to keeping brightwork intact is eliminated if the boat lives in covered moorage, or the varnished trims reside under canvas cover when the boat is not in use. I call a full boat cover the Brightwork Insurance and Retirement Plan and have calculated over and over for my clients the value of this program in dollars, time, and physical energy

units saved over the lifetime of the ownership of their boats. In addition, *hundreds* of calendar days throughout that tenure are converted from "refinishing time" to "sailing time." And what, I always ask, *is* the whole purpose in owning a boat?

One caveat about full covers: make sure they afford adequate ventilation, or you will return to a boat covered with mildew, and possibly even corrosion of electrical wiring!

option B: *you wave the magic checkbook over the finish*

CHOOSING THE FINISHER

You can have anyone, from your kid to your neighbor to the local varnishing celebrity, do the brightwork for you.

Your choice of finishing proxy is determined by three qualifiers:
1. The quality of job desired
2. The size of the refinishing budget
3. The availability of professional talent

As your taste in quality rises, so does the budget . . . just as with champagne. If you think the person who charges $5 an hour is a bargain, think again. That "pro" will typically deliver a varnish headache that has you kissing the ring of one who charges at least seven times the minimum wage, when the real brightwork artist is called in to clean up the bargain refinisher's mess . . . provided the mess can *be* cleaned up and permanent damage has

not been done. I witnessed the complete destruction of the teak veneer bulkhead on a gentleman's Cheoy Lee one summer after his girlfriend had taken an orbital sander with 80-grit paper to it, good intentions on her part converging with a desire on his to circumvent the cost of professional labor. With her good intentions she paved the road to the end of the relationship. For his part, the value got was the bargain sought. I felt sad for them both, but saddest for that beautiful boat.

WHEN YOU HIRE A PROFESSIONAL

- Ask around for referrals until three people recommend the same person.
- Don't hire someone solely on the basis of recommendation. *Look* at their prior work to determine their qualification.
- Ask their current and/or former clients how professionally they conducted the project, and whether it was done in a reasonable amount of time and within the bid or estimates given.
- Expect—no, demand—a contract, complete with bid, or at least an estimate with a cost-overruns cap.
- Payment for the work is best meted out somewhere along these lines: 25 percent deposit at start; 25 percent due upon completion of prep sanding; 25 percent due after fourth coat; balance due upon completion of project. (Of course, the nature of your own contract will vary with the type of work being done. But this is a good starting formula.)
- Treat your finishing team like royalty. Take them brownies during the project, and express your undying gratitude for their labors.

whether you choose Option A or Option B, recognize the heart of brightwork

*C*OMMITMENT to the finish program, and to your ultimate role as caring steward of your ship

*O*RGANIZATION in doing the brightwork, in knowing its place on the master to-do list, in anticipating the rhythm of finish decline

*E*NERGY as the primary currency of accomplishment, whether you do the work yourself or appoint a surrogate to do it for you

*U*NDERSTANDING the finishing subject (the wood) as well as its relationship to the finishing medium

*R*EALISTIC EXPECTATIONS with regard to the purpose, as well as limitations, of any brightwork finish

chapter **3**

**now, about
varnish—in a nutshell**

What's the basic formula? *Varnishes and solvents, briefly!*

Varnish is the *grande dame* of the brightwork coatings empire. Do you know her lineage? It's a regal evolutionary course, one spelled out in great detail in *Brightwork*. Spend an evening getting to know her and her ancient forebears and I think you will open each can of varnish thereafter with an added measure of reverence.

For the purposes of this book, the following is a perfect quick introduction to the varnish family:

OIL	+	RESIN	+	SOLVENT	=	varnish
OIL	+	RESIN	+	SOLVENT	=	oil finish
OIL	+	RESIN	+	SOLVENT	=	sealer

See the resemblances? Notice the differences?

These members of the same family attain their individual identities according to the PROPORTION of the three ingredients found within each finish.

The more resin, with a medium oil content and less solvent, the greater the buildup per coat and the likelier the finish is meant to dry and harden by simple oxidation, resulting in a deep, impervious skin. This is the coating named varnish.

The more oil, with a medium solvent content and less resin, the slower to dry, and therefore the greater the likelihood that you are applying a finish meant to be soaked on, wet-sanded, and/or buffed dry to a thin, slightly impervious film. This is varnish's little sister, the oil finish.

The more solvent, with conservative portions of both oil and resin, the likelier you are applying a finish meant solely as a prep coat for varnish, or an "impending rain" insurance coat, designed to dry almost immediately as the solvent evaporates. In this can is the baby of the family, the sealer.

Understand this essential relationship between the varnish ingredients, and you will better understand how to work with any of the finishes you choose.

Additionally, the *types* of oils, resins, and solvents employed in making varnish produce myriad variations on each type of finish.

Oddly, there is still much confusion in the world over what comprises each of these basic components.

alkyd ▪ phenolic ▪ polyurethane ▪ epoxy . . . these are R E S I N S
oititica ▪ linseed ▪ tung . . . these are O I L S
mineral spirits ▪ naphtha ▪ Japan drier . . . these are SOLVENTS

Better-quality oils—tung oil, for example—and resins—phenolics and polyurethanes both—heighten the abrasion resistance and overall tenacity of a finish and give varnish the ability to expand and contract over a piece of wood that is constantly moving, expanding, and contracting. The more solids, or resin, used in a varnish, the thicker the varnish. The thinnest varnishes right out of the can are typically cheaper, because solvent is the least expensive ingredient in the mix. Epifanes is a high-solids varnish that pours like cold honey. It is not cheap.

All varnishes and oil-finish products today also contain additives that make them proprietary and force them to behave with certain calculable manners. The best modern varnishes are ones that contain—in addition to resin, oil, and solvent—a highly developed "UV package" along with metallic driers. The UV package is a mélange of ultraviolet absorbers, antioxidants, and surface stabilizers. Without these, varnishes tend to check, erode, and fail in a shorter period of time. The metallic driers serve as catalyzing agents to hasten the setting time of the finish.

One important note on metallic driers: as varnish sits aging *in the can,* the metallic driers begin to lose their catalytic power, and the varnish will no longer dry in the designed time. Buy only as much varnish as you anticipate using within one season, and invest in fresh cans the next, even if it means wasting some leftover varnish. Better to pass along your remainders to dock mates using the same product.

a few words on solvents

The simplest and earliest varnishes contained oils and resins alone. Over time, solvents were added to the mix to accommodate application conditions. This third ingredient in the varnish formula has become the corner bar in the finishing world, the Cheers in the Boston of brightwork. Even when using the most highly respected varnishes, people think a solvent is the best way to slide through the sticky situations they find themselves in.

If the weatherman is predicting a scorcher, these folks inebriate the contents of the varnishing pot with a ton of "brushing liquid" instead of confining their varnishing efforts to the wee cool hours of the morning (the double dry martini for the CEO facing indictment). They commit to a project too late in the year and find themselves desperate to apply that last coat of varnish right before the snow flies, so they toss in a big splash of Interlux 216 to give the work more than the proverbial snowball's chance of drying (a nice triple espresso for lunch after too late a night out on the town). Some people take extreme measures, dumping in Japan drier when they feel like forcing the drying issue (a hit of speed, a raw egg in tomato juice, some hair of the dog, and the triple espresso after partying hard five nights straight). You might get away with these things, but sometimes at a cost to the body of the finish.

I'm always amazed when I watch someone open one of the most popular, and thickest, varnishes, for which they have shelled out a pretty penny, then proceed to thin it 50 percent just so they can brush it on—and that's on the fourth coat! It's thick for a reason: its full body is the character of the varnish. If you buy a high-solids varnish, learn how to *apply* such a varnish. If you aren't experienced enough to brush out something that has the consistency of cold honey, save your money and buy a less viscous varnish, and apply it as close to full strength as conditions allow. For your efforts you end up with a coat with integrity and haven't thoroughly diluted your varnish—and *time*—investment.

My advice across the board (so to speak!) is to follow the wisdom of the inscrutable F. Maire, quoted in chapter 1. If a product is not satisfactory coming from the factory, how is even the most professional finisher the more capable varnish mixologist? Buy a reputable varnish, use it according to the manufacturer's instructions, use the solvents packaged by that manufacturer for recommended manipulation of application circumstances, and employ common sense in applying that finish to your boat. In that way, the odds are on your side that you will be calling it "the best varnish."

part **2** the
refinishing
program

chapter **4**

order

in the port!

Time is precious. Outsmart the clock by being organized . . .

there are three governors in every brightwork artist's life:

1. the master to-do list

2. the weather

3. the materials inventory

(. . . and then there's that little business about an organized boat)

the master to-do list
thirteen beautification projects

In "deductive destructive order," the following are cosmetic projects you may be facing at any one time on your boat.

If you make every effort to tackle these projects in this order, you lessen the risk of ruining subsequent work on the list.

1. Sanding and painting the bottom
2. Repainting or varnishing spars
3. Sanding painted topsides and/or above decks to prep for repainting
4. Bleaching deck and brightwork to remove oil finishes
5. Stripping brightwork with heat, dry scrapers, or sandpaper
6. Chemical stripping of varnish or paint above decks
7. Bleaching to clean up bare decks and weathered trims
8. Sanding, oiling, and/or varnishing brightwork
9. Painting topsides and above decks
10. Sanding bleached decks
11. Waxing topsides
12. Polishing bronze or other metal fixtures
13. Painting decks

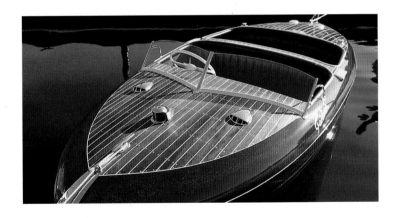

rebecca's first law
of brightwork dominion:
organize projects according to the weather, and you're guaranteed to finish them within your lifetime

In the hierarchy of organizing projects around the weather, start first with seasonal organization:

SPRING—when it's frequently raining . . . is the best time for exterior bleaching, because the air is cool and moist. Sometimes you get lucky and can get started on other exterior projects like painting and varnishing (depending on your latitude). It's a lovely time to varnish interiors, especially cabin soles.

SUMMER—when it's often sunny . . . is when it's easiest to bank on completion of exterior work of all kinds, which is why so many people set aside entire blocks of vacation time in July to work on their boats. This accounts for the high vacancy rate in the cruising marinas during that month.

FALL—when mother nature is still fooling herself . . . is a good time to wrap up, as quickly as possible, any uncompleted exterior finishing business, and focus on projects belowdecks that require strong ventilation and open hatches (wholesale varnishing and oiling, for example)

WINTER—when the mercury dips below 45°F . . . is the time to take projects to the shop or confine interior projects to light oiling, or the perfect time to just curl up with a nice book. How about *Brightwork: The Art of Finishing Wood?*

And since nobody—at least nobody in *our* employ—controls the keys to the weather, the next best thing is to outsmart the weather. Organize projects around both the weather that is predicted and the weather that happens.

(Everyone knows these are two completely different kinds of weather . . .)

- Plan your project according to what the meteorologist predicts for *the morning of the work.*
- Always plan a contingency project on the boat, in the very slight event that predictions prove false.
- Know how to read the clouds as the day progresses.
- Pray for a pair of Dutchman's pants in every cloudy sky.

Learning to outsmart the weather is critical to completing brightwork projects within the finishing seasons. Always save portable parts of the project for last, and if a surprise downpour stops work at the boat, take a piece of the boat home and continue there. For example, if you have detachable Dorade boxes or cockpit grates, save them for the end of each phase, and concentrate your initial good-weather hours on the toerail and butterfly hatches. Or, if you are doing exterior *and* interior work all within the same time frame, allow the exterior trims to command all your attention first. If you never get rained out, bully for you; if you do, you're still on schedule.

The best little source for reading clouds: *Instant Weather Forecasting* by Alan Watts. Keep this book—always—in your tool bag.

And what ARE Dutchman's pants?

As long as even the tiniest patch of blue peeks out between the clouds, regardless of whether it's been raining or rain is rumored to be impending, the presence of a "Dutchman's pants" foretells a clearing of the skies. This is a folk tale that just happens to be more reliable than the weatherman.

the brightwork materials imperative:
shop once!

Or at least not eighty-three times during the course of one varnishing project.

Nothing wastes time like running to the chandlery for a sheet of sandpaper. Or a new tack cloth. Or *one* more foam brush. Having a full materials inventory also gives you flexibility to shift to another phase if something torpedoes your original plan for the day.

Shopping once means having a firm grasp of:

- the type of finish you plan to use
- which mode of stripping the old finish dictates
- what actual materials you need to complete each phase
- how much of everything it takes to complete the lion's share of the project

Buy in bulk if the scope of your project even slightly warrants doing so. Sandpaper is much cheaper purchased by the sleeve than by the sheet; foam brushes make a lot more sense purchased by the box than by the brush. These things don't "go bad" if you don't use them immediately.

Shop smart

- Call your materials order in to the "will-call desk" and avoid waiting in line behind nine other people.
- Gauge what materials are low at the end of each weekend, and buy replacement supplies before you run out.
- Organize a cooperative of dock mates, and have each person sign up for a week as "materials runner."

And one last little thing before launching into a refinishing project . . .

order in the port! *organize the boat!*

Turn your dreamboat into a floating theme park of efficiency:

- **strip off every fitting** that stands in the refinishing path
- **dismantle "portables"** (*anything* not built in!) for finishing at dockside or for "shop time" on rainy days

Your best friends in this operation:

- A variable speed/reversible drill—which you employ in removing fasteners
- Ziploc bags and a Sharpie laundry marker—where you place and label each individual piece of hardware *and its fasteners*
- A map—which you make of the boat as you chart the source of each piece of hardware upon removal

Do not dispense with the map and simply toss everything into a bucket. You will be sorry if you do that. Trust me.

- **stow or protect all lines and canvas covers** that could suffer from refinishing fallout

you've named the finish;

you've shopped;

the weather is right;

the boat is bare;

your loved ones are all happy . . .

Get to work!

chapter **5**

**strip me once,
strip me twice,
strip me once again,
it's been a long, long time...**

there are essentially two types of coatings in the brightwork world: *hard & penetrating*

A HARD FINISH is any varnish or paint finish that is built up to create a skin, and can include anything from a phenolic formula to an epoxy finish.

PENETRATING FINISHES are those coatings that, despite repeated applications, do not build up to form a skin; these can include any oil, silicone, or other coating that literally penetrates the wood. With these types of finishes, there are five basic methods for removal: acid bleaching, heat guns, chemical strippers, dry-scraping, and sanding. A brightwork artist may face any combination of these coatings within one restoration project, and should understand all the stripping options when choosing a path to bare wood surfaces.

STRIPPING METHOD	FINISH IT CAN REMOVE	DEGREE OF DIFFICULTY	RJW'S RATING	
Acid bleaching system (TE-KA A&B)	Oil, silicone sealers, Deks Olje #1 & 2	Easy, but with big caveats	10	Speedy, efficient
Heat gun	Most hard finishes, including Sikkens Cetol	Easy, with practice	10	Efficient, cost effective
Chemical remover	Standard hard finishes and some epoxy coatings	Requires patience to get results	5	Costly, messy, time-consuming
Dry-scraping	Any hard finish	Requires a sure hand, strong body, flat plane	3	Not a method for amateurs
Sanding	Any finish	Not a smart way to strip	1	Only as a last resort

how to: *bleach off a finish*

THE TE-KA A&B BLEACHING SYSTEM was designed nominally for use on teak, but it can be deployed on everything from teak to mahogany to cedar to ironbark to remove an oil finish. In an easy two-step treatment, a ghastly failed oil finish, along with blackened mildew, disappears like magic. Te-Ka A&B can also strip off a tired Deks Olje #2 coating, if what remains of that finish is relatively thin and broken down.

MATERIALS

Te-Ka A&B Bleach
(gallon sets, plus a quart set for each person working)

Clean retired diapers

A source of fresh water

TOOLS

3M soft (white) nylon scrubbers

Soft-bristle toothbrushes

Large plastic funnel

Water hose with spray nozzle

Roll of duct tape and 4-mil plastic sheeting

SAFETY GEAR

Emergency eye-wash kit

Construction rain gear

Nitrile gloves

Kneepads (for deck work)

Deck boots

Eye shields

optimal weather

Cool, overcast is divine

Sunny or misty is OK

No torrential rains!

recommended crew

A crew of two is critical to staying sane on large jobs

attire

The construction rain suit: you're a stranger in your own pants!

The company that makes Te-Ka A&B prints a warning label on each bottle that reads "Te-Ka should be used only on teak and must not be applied on any other type of surface." This is their way of escaping liability for the havoc the bleach can wreak on things like paint, gelcoat, and metallic surfaces, among others. Completing a number of organizational tasks makes it possible to circumvent that admonition. Skip any one that is germane to your project, however, and you will rue the day you bought the product.

organizing

the boat: Protect painted topsides, the boat's name, or any other vulnerable area by using a bleaching skirt: attach an apron of 4-mil clear plastic sheeting (available by the roll at hardware stores)—using duct tape—at the base of the toerail, below the scuppers (or just below the wood being bleached), encircling the entire boat. If there is a danger of the duct tape pulling up a painted topside finish, run a strip of 3M Safe Release tape (see Taping in chapter 13) along the top edge where the duct tape would otherwise initially adhere to the hull, then attach the skirt as described. Test the skirt for leaks with a thorough spraying of the bleaching areas before beginning the work.

Take any portable pieces of the boat slated for bleaching to the dock, especially cockpit grates, companionway boards, or Dorade boxes (just remember to seal the openings!). Any *vulnerable* items that you do not wish to mar—including anodized aluminum whisker poles or bronze appointments—*must* either be taken off the boat or wrapped carefully with plastic and sealed off from exposure to the bleach. At the very least, if these protective measures cannot be taken (as is the case with an anodized aluminum toerail, for example), a thick coating of carnauba wax is imperative to prevent scoring of the anodized finish. Make sure all hatches, portholes, vents, and other miscellaneous openings are closed and tightly secured. Remove all lines from the deck (you can pile them atop the mainsail), and remove all deck-level canvas covers from resident locations.

the crew: Another of those things that Te-Ka should not be used on is skin or any part of one's body. No crew member should begin the job—even filling work bottles—without first donning nitrile gloves, eye shields, deck boots, and knee pads, and then slipping into a protective rain suit.

the materials and equipment: Set up a bottle-filling station; dockside is best. Always refill working sets (quart bottles) from gallons. Working with gallon bottles is unwieldy and ultimately wastes a lot of product. Assign a toothbrush, a nylon scrubbing pad, and a set of Te-Ka to each crew member.

caveats: Never use bristle scrub brushes, coarse scrubbing pads, or brass wire brushes, or you will end up destroying the pith of the grain. And on that note, don't scrub with a vengeance, even with a soft pad; allow the chemistry to do the work for you. To get the most for your Te-Ka money, don't be a miser in your applications of the A (bleach) or B (neutralizer) solutions. The system is truly effective only when it reaches the wood full strength, and will betray streaky application in a sketchily divested finish. A poorly neutralized bleaching will leave the wood dark and looking chemically burned.

doing the work

1. Read labels on the product for basic application procedures. Test the product and your bleaching skills on a small area first.

2. Before you begin actual bleaching, give the entire boat (or piece you're working on) a good dousing. Then—in the case of the boat—check to make sure all drains and scuppers are clear for proper runoff during the work. If you find that the boat is leaking water belowdecks, better to stop the work and resolve the leaks first; otherwise, you will face an unholy mess later with bleach everywhere below.

3. Start at the highest point on the boat and plan your attack "downstream" from there. Working in the opposite direction wastes a ton of the neutralizer (B) and adds unnecessary time to the work.

4. Apply the bleach (A) solution first, spreading it evenly with the nylon pad (not scrubbing), leaving *no* voids. Let this application sit until it has saturated the wood (turning it alarmingly black!); then apply a second coating before you begin to scrub.

5. When you've finished scrubbing, push aside most of the slimy goo to create a clearer surface for the neutralizer. As you apply the B, scrub lightly—especially around detail work—using the nylon pad or soft toothbrushes to dislodge all the softened finish scum. You will know you have sufficiently neutralized the wood when it has returned to its natural golden tone. Any spots that are still black require additional neutralizing and should be given repeated squirts of B until they come up light.

6. Allow the neutralizer to sit about ten minutes after it has turned the wood golden, and then start rinsing off the entire bleached surface and all surrounding dirty runoff. As you rinse, scrub the recesses again, gently, to dislodge any scum.

7. Water is your greatest ally in this project. Keep a constant stream running down the gunwales to dilute unneutralized runoff. If you're working on a warm day, shoot a periodic mist over treated areas to prevent the solutions from drying out.

8. When the entire project is complete, elevate any docking lines that rest on bleached wood. Rinse the boat for at least twenty minutes and then conduct "bleed-back" patrol, looking for recesses that release, belatedly, unneutralized bleach. These will be apparent as darkened areas, usually around seams and joints, and can be fixed with a little shot of straight neutralizer left to sit overnight.

wrapping up

When all danger of bleed-back has passed, give the boat one last rinse. Dismantle the bleaching skirt, rinse the topsides and spars, and give the entire boat a good looking-over for leaks, standing puddles of bleach, and latent scum.

If you've bleached a deck and there are surrounding stretches of healthy, varnished brightwork, wipe the varnished surfaces dry before leaving the boat for the day. This prevents water spotting of the finish.

Allow the bleached wood to dry thoroughly (6 to 24 hours, depending on the type of wood and overall temperature) before sanding or commencing any further steps in the refinishing program.

how to: *strip with a heat gun*

Stripping with a heat gun is the quickest, cleanest, easiest, and most socially responsible method of finish removal. And it's a kick, once you get the hang of it. It will save you hundreds of finishing dollars and untold labor hours, and once you've completed your work at the boat, you'll discover that the ugly painted trims in your home are now fair game with this weapon at your side. The keys are owning the right heat gun and patience (in learning to use it). Make sure the heat gun you use heats up to *at least* 1,100°F, or you'll have a slow go of it.

Have fun!

TOOLS

Heat gun

Hook scrapers

A fine mill file

SAFETY GEAR

Dust masks

Nitrile gloves

Knee pads

EQUIPMENT

Vacuum cleaner with brush nozzle attachment

Extension cord and a source of electrical power

optimal weather

Mild climate, cool to hot; no strong winds or rain

recommended crew

One-man job, but a helper gets you a conversation

attire

No ostrich feather boas

organizing

the boat: Make sure the boat and all finishes slated for stripping are dry. Remove all impediments to your work; coil lines and stow all extraneous items away from the work area. If stripping areas are directly adjacent to painted surfaces not meant for refinishing, affix a thin batten along the painted boundary or have a helper slide one along as you strip those areas.

the crew: If heat-scraping is a new experience for you or your helpers, have everyone doing the work practice first on something that is not the boat: an old chair or dresser. Get a feel for the heat/scrape rhythm that parts the finish from the wood. Rehearse burning finishes right down to the wood, and figure out when to pull the heat gun up as the finish softens, before the wood is charred.

the equipment: Sharpen all the scrapers (AWAY FROM AND DOWNWIND OF THE BOAT). See A Tool Tip on page 54 for information about proper sharpening. Set up the extension cord, belaying it at a stanchion if plugged in at the dock. Park the vacuum near the targeted work area and connect the heat gun to the extension cord, joining them in a square knot at the plug.

Use some imagination when amassing scraping tools for use with a heat gun. Do not, however, use a putty knife, chisel, or any type of scraper that requires a pushing motion, or invariably the wood will end up gouged. Besides the standard assortment of scrapers, my heat-stripping tool bag carries everything from dental picks to antique penknives.

caveats: Stripping action will diminish even in a mild breeze. If you cannot avoid slightly windy conditions, erect a windbreak around your work. Don't bear down on the scraper; too much pressure dulls the blade and gouges the wood. If you must scrape across the grain, do so delicately or you risk ripping the grain. Scrape around bungs carefully, in the same way you would cross-grain.

doing the work

1. Start with the most challenging areas at the beginning of each day, reserving the easier spots for later when energy is flagging.

2. To strip, hold the gun in your secondary hand, aim the nozzle at the wood at a 45-degree angle and about an inch from the surface, and heat for about 5 seconds or until the finish begins to bubble, whichever comes first. Flip the heat up, away from the wood, and immediately begin scraping, by firmly pulling the hook scraper toward you, across the full length of softened finish. Repeat in successive stretches. Expect occasionally to make more than one heat pass at stubborn patches until the finish releases.

3. When you develop some proficiency at using the heat gun, you'll discover that, rather than flipping the gun up and away as you scrape, you'll be able to coordinate heating a subsequent stretch as you scrape off the earlier one. This will speed the process considerably.

4. Vacuum varnish flakes as they begin to pile up near your work. They can be a fire hazard if in the line of ignition, and at best will slow down the stripping process. If the wind kicks up and they go fluttering into the waterways, you could also face a pollution fine.

wrapping up

Any varnish that remains in the pores, along with residual paste wood filler and/or stain, can be dispatched in the course of prep sanding or with chemical finish remover (see next section). Otherwise, if the wood seems thoroughly stripped, give the boat a final vacuuming to capture the last of the varnish flakes, and then move on to sanding and surface prep measures.

notes

a tool tip!

Your ability to scrape efficiently is commensurate with the condition of your blade. Sharpening a scraper is an art in itself. The goal is twofold: maintain a scraper edge bevel that is a 35- to 45-degree angle, then keep a solid burr on the flat underside (the scraping edge) of the bevel. This can be accomplished with practice when applied to hook scraper blades. Use a fine mill file for maintaining the bevel: then, turning the mill file on its smooth side edge, press firmly along the edge to turn a burr down on the freshly sharpened bevel. You'll know you've created a sufficient burr by reading it with your thumb: strokes up from under the burr should meet with a nice drag against the end of the blade. If the underside feels smooth all the way off the edge, you need to work it some more until that drag is achieved.

For further elucidation, and an illustrated explanation of the sharpening art as it applies to all kinds of blades, buy a classic little book on the use and care of planes and scrapers entitled Planecraft by C. W. Hampton and E. Clifford. It sells for $9.95 from Woodcraft Supply Company. You can order it by calling 800 225 1153 or writing to the company at 10 State Street, Box 4000, Woburn, Massachusetts 01888.

how to: *remove finishes that require chemical strippers*

If there were but one reason to rewrite *Brightwork,* this would be it.

There is now a product on the market that supplants all my previous recommendations and instructions for the use of methylene chloride strippers. This new product (which, at this printing, isn't really so new) makes it possible to leave off the list below such items as lacquer thinner, neoprene-coated gloves, and the "air-supplied respirator." It renders moot all admonishments about the dangers of solvent intoxication and mandates for strong ventilation. It smells delicious, works beautifully, doesn't cost a fortune, and doesn't force our guests from the job site. I wish I owned the company. It's called Citristrip, and I'll bet you've seen it at your local home improvement emporium (if you haven't, turn to chapter 13 to find out how to track it down).

MATERIALS

Citristrip stripping gel

Soft toothbrushes

3M soft Scotch-Brite pad

Gallon-size paper buckets

Clean shop rags

3M Solvent Resistant Tape

6-mil plastic sheeting and newspapers

Heavy-duty paper towels

TOOLS

Wide plastic or hardwood scrapers

1- to 4-inch chip brushes

Large plastic tub

Fresh water

SAFETY GEAR

Nitrile gloves

Eye shields or protection

optimal weather

Mild temps best; no rain or wind

recommended crew

Nice meditative project for one person

attire

Full armor is wise; chain mail optional

organizing

the boat: The sorts of trims and appointments that require the use of a chemical stripper in lieu of a heat gun are typically pieces that are moderately ornate and not solidly affixed to the boat and that can often be parted from their station at the turn of a nut. The helm is a popular candidate for chemical stripper. Louvered doors are another, though many times a creative choice of scraper with a heat gun can do the job there. At any rate, if it is possible, take the piece to be stripped *off* the boat and do it in your shop or garage. If the piece is not portable, set up several layers of heavy-mil plastic, topped with newspapers, to catch the drips.

the crew: Issue eye shields and nitrile gloves to anyone working on this job. Citristrip might be highly user friendly, but it's still caustic to skin. I also like to don an old men's dress shirt—XL—to protect my clothes during this messy task.

the materials and equipment: Set up a work station: place the piece to be stripped, along with the Citristrip, scraping tools, brushes, and paper buckets, on a "tablecloth" of plastic and several layers of newspaper. Run water into the plastic tub about 3 inches deep and set the toothbrushes and Scotch-Brite pad next to it.

caveats: This product will eat paint. If you are stripping trims adjacent to painted surfaces, protect those areas with solvent-resistant tape (see chapter 13).

doing the work

1. Apply a liberal coating of stripper to the wood and work it generously into nooks and crannies. This is best done by pouring straight from the container and spreading with the chip brushes. Make several passes until you have a thick, unbroken layer of stripper in place.

2. Allow the stripper to stand, undisturbed on the wood, for at least twenty minutes or until the solution seems to begin drying out. If and when that happens, apply another coating of

stripper. Repeat this until the stripper no longer dries out when left to stand for approximately half an hour.

3. When you think the finish is thoroughly softened, test-scrape a spot. If the wood seems to be completely denuded, work the finish out of the filigreed areas with the toothbrush, and then scrape up all the dregs and dump them into the paper buckets. Try to contain all drips and spills as you scrape. Use paper towels to wipe off dregs that elude the scraper.

4. Rinse the stripping residue from the piece with plain water, gently scrubbing with the Scotch-Brite pad. When the piece is thoroughly cleaned, wipe it dry with shop towels.

5. Inspect for unstripped areas, and repeat the above steps until the entire piece is bare.

wrapping up

Don't pour these materials down the drain or into the trash.

Dispose of the dregs according to the recommendations of your local waste management agencies. If you are stripping a boat that is currently floating, make darned sure you contain the dregs. As seemingly innocuous as this stripper is, it is highly illegal to drop it into waterways.

notes

how to: *dry-scrape . . . if you must*

If there is some expansive stretch of wood that needs to be stripped to beneath the surface (the one valid reason for choosing this method), dry-scraping can be the speedier way to peel back the finish. This exhausting method, however, takes many hours of practice to arrive at a proficiency that hedges the risks involved. The greatest risk looming over the scraper-wielding stripper is the possibility of gashing the wood with a poorly executed swipe. Once that happens, you negate any perceived benefit in savings of time and dollars as you take on a greater sanding burden, if the error can *be* sanded out. Consider going another route if at all possible.

TOOLS

Heavy-duty scraper

Fine mill file

EQUIPMENT

Vacuum with brush nozzle attachment

Extension cord and a source of
    electrical power

SAFETY GEAR

Dust mask

Nitrile gloves

optimal weather

Anything that doesn't involve foulies

recommended crew

Many *capable* hands make . . . light work

attire

A sweatband is good; clothes avert openly
    brutal derision

organizing

the boat: Your boat is your oyster. Set it up any way you like.

the crew: Helpers just need to promise to love you the next day when they're too stiff to move.

the materials and equipment: Sharpen scrapers. Provide high-energy fuel for the crew. Water, tons of it, is important. Gatorade is a godsend in the heat.

caveats: See introductory paragraph. Trims and rails can lose their shape from wholesale dry-scraping, and necessitate greater sanding later to resculpt the curves.

doing the work

1. Make sure your scraper is sharp. Use a fine mill file to create the appropriate burr on a good, steel-bladed hook-style scraper (preferably with a handle designed for additional pressure from your secondary hand). Resharpen the scraper repeatedly throughout the work whenever the honed edge loses its burr. Remember: sharpen downwind and away from the boat!

2. Hold the scraper at a slight angle to the grain of the wood, bear down a bit, and pull toward you in a firm, even-handed, level stroke.

3. Make sure you have excellent light when you do the work, to help you see bungs, joints, and cross-grain areas. Scrape carefully around these spots, where you risk tearing up the grain.

4. Vacuum the mess of scrapings that accrues as you go, bearing in mind that many marinas have antipollution laws that prohibit the introduction of even teak dust into the waterways.

wrapping up

When finished, vacuum well. Plan a three-phase sanding to reshape, smooth, and define the wood prior to finishing.

how to: (know when and how to) *sand a finish off*

The only part of a boat you should be crazy enough to strip with *sandpaper* is one that is just absolutely not accessible by heat gun or scraper and that cannot, for whatever reason, be stripped chemically. I believe I've run into such a spot *once* in all my days of finishing brightwork. It was a previously varnished deck, and I was determined to strip this horror to the farthest reaches of the cockpit, including all the way back underneath a suspended lazarette, which provided a working clearance of about three inches.

Because God forbid I, the consummate professional, should leave the varnish unstripped *there* and have to face myself in the mirror with the unmerciful guilt of having *skipped a spot,* even though *nobody* whose face wasn't wrenched into position, contorted at deck level right in front of that area could possibly see that the old finish had been left in place. *Nobody. Ever . . .* (My mother says she thinks the therapy is beginning to help . . .)

For that *once* in your brightwork finishing lifetime, here are a few tips to speed you through your own little bouts of lunacy.

MATERIALS

2-inch 3M #2040 masking tape

50-grit 3M Production sandpaper

60-grit 3M Fre-Cut sandpaper

TOOLS

Sandpaper cutter

Steel cabinet scraper

Steel putty knife (wide)

SAFETY GEAR

Nitrile gloves

Dust masks

EQUIPMENT

Vacuum with crevice tool and brush nozzle attachment

Extension cord and a source of electrical power

optimal weather

Sunny, just like your disposition

recommended crew

A good job for unskilled friends who wish to earn a sailing invitation

attire

Crawl-space couture

organizing

the boat: Run a double layer of masking tape along any gel-coat or painted surface abutting the area to be sanded. If you skip this, you (or your client) will be very unhappy later, when you vacuum up the dust and discover the brutal effects of heavy grit on innocent neighboring finishes.

the crew: Encourage everyone to see this as a brief hardship. Lessen their pain by enforcing the requirement to wear dust masks and gloves.

the materials and equipment: Cut sandpaper into quarters, then make trifolds (see page 65), or wrap sandpaper around a cabinet scraper and/or putty knife and tape tightly in place.

caveats: Your only concerns should revolve around unwanted scratching of adjacent surfaces, with maybe the added risk of throwing your back out as you squeeze yourself into some ridiculously tight space. Take my advice: if you can't *see* this area, let it go . . .

doing the work

1. Sand, in whatever way accomplishes your goal, using as much imagination as you can muster and employing common sense in deciding when enough is enough.

2. Vacuum as you go, using the crevice tool, to help keep the work visible and extend the life of the sandpaper.

3. Try not to sand across the grain, but if you must in order to get results and the results are visible, soften the scars with finishing grits later.

wrapping up

Vacuum thoroughly, and ponder the wisdom of a finish in that spot in the first place. Chances are, if it couldn't be accessed in a reasonable fashion for stripping, it's equally inaccessible to the human eye. A finish in such a place is rarely functioning as vital protector, which leaves misplaced vanity as the only impetus for varnishing.

it's a
thankless job,
and your name
is Somebody

intermediate prep work

In fine finishing everywhere, the most frequently articulated fact is the importance of a good prep job.

Gloss over this critical phase of the work and you risk compromising not just the appearance but the life of the finish.

intermediate prep work has three distinct functions:

SHAPING to restore the design of a piece that has been stripped

REPAIRING the surface defects of the piece

CLARIFYING the wood grain to maximize its countenance beneath a new finish.

To achieve those ends, one needs to know the

intermediate prep how-to's . . .

- sanding wood
- bleaching out surface stains
- creating a smooth brightwork plane
- finding God (and *not* the Devil) in the details

how to: *sand bare wood*

In the brightwork world, there are two ways to sand:

BY HAND . . .

employing:
- elbow grease
- assorted hand-sanding aids
- trifold quarters

BY MACHINE . . .

employing:
- orbital finishing sanders
- random orbit sanders (ROS)
- detail sanders

. . . and hey!!

a sandpaper tip!

3M Fre-Cut sandpaper is the only sandpaper appropriate for use in brightwork. This is the grade of sandpaper implied throughout every project described in this book, except in wet-sanding of oil finishes. (See chapter 13.)

When starting with stripped wood, work progressively through each of the sanding phases to reach a mirror finish.

In areas inaccessible by machine (louvers, for example), we're often inclined to sand through the phases by hand. There, *detail sanders* can sometimes be used. (See page 143 on Fein sanders.)

THERE ARE FOUR PHASES OF SANDING	1) SHAPING	2) FINISHING	3) CLARIFYING	4) BETWEEN COATS
achieved with the following grit ranges	60–80–100	120–150	220	220–320–400
which is best accomplished by	Orbital or ROS	Orbital or ROS	Orbital or ROS	Hand
which delivers a surface that is	Grain flattened, shape restored	Free of sander swirls, scars	Clear grained, smooth	Progressively faired to a mirror finish

another sandpaper tip!

what is a trifold quarter?

Maximize the life of your sandpaper, and get the most for your 3M dollar, by cutting each full sheet into quarters and then folding each quarter sheet into threes, one third overlapping the other. In this way, the paper doesn't slip around during hand-sanding, and the grits aren't rubbing one another off before they get a stab at the wood.

and a message from your body . . .

Wood dust is a scientifically proven *carcinogen*. There is nothing macho or smart about sanding without the protection of a dust mask (not a "particle mask," which, per an unnamed 3M source, is but worthless proxy for your nose hairs). *Wear a particulate respirator, commonly referred to as a dust mask.* (See chapter 13 for the best brand and model.) Your lungs will thank you, as will your adoring children.

a dozen and one sanding tips

- Never sand next to a painted or gelcoated surface without masking to protect that surface. Double the tape when sanding by machine.

- Never employ a belt sander on brightwork trims and furniture, and use one on decks only if you are highly experienced with that sander.

- Never skip the finishing and clarifying phases of sanding. The heavy-grit scratches will come back to haunt you on the first coat of varnish.

- Never sand a veneer by machine, and never use anything coarser than 220 grit to prep veneers for a finish.

- Always load an orbital sander with multiple sheets to reduce time spent changing worn-out sandpaper (see chapter 12).

- Machine-sand as much of the work as possible. But treat the broad surfaces to a pass by hand after each of the phases, to abate sander swirls.

- Complete all the work for each grit before moving to the next phase; do machine work first and then handwork, always in that order.

- Don't sand what you should bleach; sacrificing actual wood is a mistake if all you want to do is remove gray-black surface oxidation.

- Wrap 60-grit sandpaper around a chunk of 2x4 to fair surfaces sporting bungs, or the harder bungs will stand proud of the leveled plane.

- Sand in good light at all times; if necessary, keep a lamp shining back at your project, at work level, to see how the wood is shaping up.

- As you complete each sanding phase, vacuum well and wipe the surface with mineral spirits to check for sander swirls and defects.

- When shaping wood for the first time, knock all sharp edges and corners down to a soft radius, to ensure their hold on the finish.

- Avoid sanding across the grain whenever possible. If you must, however, do so through the full range of grits to remove deep scratches.

how to: *bleach out surface stains*

Woods with marginal stores of natural oil are prone to water staining after prolonged exposure to moist air and rain. Mahogany, oak, cedar, spruce—these are commonly vulnerable woods, and when their varnish has broken down and the wood is left open to the elements, moisture begins to leave its mark. These stains are a pale shade of black and can burrow some distance into the wood.

Complete the first phase of sanding (shaping) and then attack these stains with a bleaching regimen.

If this does not remove the stains entirely, it can at the very least reduce their intensity, making them less conspicuous beneath a new finish.

MATERIALS

Oxalic acid crystals

Borax (powder)

Boiling water

Poly-Brush

Chip brushes

4-mil plastic sheeting

A source of fresh water

EQUIPMENT

Nonreactive bowl or bucket
(not stainless steel)

Wooden slotted spoon

SAFETY GEAR

Nitrile gloves

Eye shields

optimal weather

Warm or mild; no rain

recommended crew

A one-man job

attire

Christian Lacroix is out

organizing

the boat: needs to be dry and free of sanding dust; cover areas surrounding the work with 4-mil plastic, to catch runoff.

the materials and equipment: a source of nearby heat for boiling the water is critical for delivering *hot* bleach to the stains.

caveats: Once the bleaching solution begins to cool, it recrystallizes. *Do not be tempted to reheat this solution, especially in the microwave,* or you will produce toxic fumes. Throw it out and mix a new solution from scratch.

doing the work

1. For spot-bleaching: Mix oxalic acid crystals and boiling water to form a runny paste. Apply immediately to blackened area (while still hot) with a chip brush.

   For larger expanse of stains: *Dissolve* 16 ounces oxalic acid crystals in 1 gallon boiling water. Apply immediately to stained area, "painting" the solution on with a foam brush. Apply repeated coats until the solution is used up or has cooled and begins to recrystallize.

2. Allow bleach to sit, untouched, drying, on the wood for 24 hours. Cover with heavy plastic, if necessary, to protect from condensation or impending rain.

3. If *not* satisfied with the bleached results, DO NOT NEUTRAL-IZE. Apply another treatment of hot bleach, allowing it to stand another 24 hours. Repeat this drill until you are content with the outcome, and then neutralize and rinse per instructions below. However, if satisfactory results are not achieved by the second pass, realize that further treatments will make little difference in the outcome.

4. If you are satisfied with the bleached results, mix a neutralizing solution of 3 ounces borax and 1 gallon hot water and wash the area thoroughly, then rinse clean.

wrapping up

After everything is thoroughly rinsed, allow the wood to dry before moving on to the finish sanding phase of prep. Sometimes bleaching is ineffective. Certain water stains are a fact of the brightwork, especially at joints and surrounding bungs. These stains reach into the meat of the wood from prolonged wicking at the spongelike end grain. You can either learn to live with them, cut them out and scarf in new wood, or camouflage them with paint or a heavy paste stain.

how to: *create a smooth brightwork plane*

When you've completed heavy-grit sanding and any surface bleaching work on the boat, and before you move on to the finishing grits, there are prep items that ensure a more beautiful and longer-lasting finish. These steps restore the surface integrity of the wood. If you skip these details, you leave yourself not only little eyesores to ponder but the risk of earlier breakdown of the new finish.

filling voids and gaps

Varnish—I don't care what the manufacturer claims on the label—will *not* bridge that gap between scarf joints. And varnish has a difficult time sticking to many commercial wood putty products. A good way to fill those crevices and get your varnish to actually marry the wood at these joints is to fill the joints and other surface gaps with an "epoxy/wood-flour putty" you make yourself.

- Using 220-grit sandpaper, sand *by hand* in a cleanly stripped area of the wood being finished until you've produced about a half teaspoon of clean "wood flour." Carefully collect the dust and place it in a clean container (I use the underside of empty paper varnish buckets).

- Mask along the edges of the area to be filled, using 1-inch 3M #2040 masking tape (nothing lighter weight). Press the tape *firmly* along the inside edges.

- Thoroughly mix the wood flour with a packet of Hardman Double/Bubble epoxy (see chapter 13) or 1 tablespoon other two-part epoxy.

- Immediately, with a popsicle-type stick, *and working with great dispatch,* drizzle or swipe the mixture into the masked void to fill it slightly proud of level.

- As soon as the spot is full, QUICKLY—*before* the epoxy begins to gel—pull off the tape, cutting cleanly and straight along the epoxy-filled area.

- Save all the areas to be filled for one day's operation, but mix no more than 1 tablespoon putty at a time; otherwise, it is impossible to win the setting up and unmasking race. If you do end up with setting epoxy before the tape is off, *leave* the tape in place and remove it after the mixture is completely set and not rubbery; otherwise, you risk pulling soft-set epoxy out of the joint as you pull off the tape.

The important thing to remember when mixing a magic epoxy potion: the wood dust is not there just to help the glue blend in with the original wood; it's what gives the cementlike epoxy an ability to flex. Skimp on the dust and the filling will crack the first time the joint moves. Add too much dust and the glue will be too rubbery to stick. Aim for something akin to Goldilocks's favorite porridge: a mixture that's just right.

how to: *replace bungs*

As you survey the stretches of denuded brightwork before you, take a close look at the bungs, and see this as the perfect time to repair or replace ones that are not in excellent shape.

a technique for removing bungs: Drill a pilot hole in the center of the bung, and then drive in a screw. Once the screw tip fetches up on the fastener head, additional turning will force the bung upward.

getting a good seal on new bungs: The classic method for sealing a new bung is to make it fit so tightly that it seals itself at the first whiff of marine air. If that fails, some people resort to dipping the bung in varnish before they tap it into place; others like to glue bungs in with Resorcinal. That's OK. What isn't OK is setting bungs in epoxy—not unless you know you're never ever going to need to get at that fastener again.

going my way? When installing new bungs, be mindful of one oft-neglected detail: the direction of the grain. Set the grain of the bung parallel, not perpendicular or (my personal pet peeve)

cockeyed to the grain surrounding it. If you are cutting your own bungs, attempt to cut them from a piece of stock similar in grain and color to the area receiving them. If you're dealing with a variety of hues, cut an assortment of bungs to accommodate that range, and place them in the wood accordingly. In doing things this way, you earn the title "Artist."

know in advance what color the new bung will be once it's varnished: How can I tell, you ask? Dip it in some mineral spirits, wipe solvent over the area meant to hold that bung, and compare the two. If it's a match (and unless you're going for the "calico surprise" . . .), tap it in!

but what if the old bung has just a little tiny chip missing? Don't sweat the little tiny things. Call it a "feature." (See, Mom? The therapy *is* working . . .) But if it holds your attention past 5 seconds, add this to the joint-filling project described on pages 70–71. Topping up the small divots just nets you a fairer varnished plane in the end.

when it comes to brightwork: *God* **(and not the Devil)** *is in the details . . .*

how to: *do the preparatory detailing*

If the *last* person who did the brightwork on your boat left a bank of encrusted varnish scum, teak oil spilled into the nonskid, and nasty varnish runs all over the hull, clean up this mess *before* you proceed with new finish application. This prepares all the adjacent surfaces for a clean varnish bond and eliminates postvarnish detailing that could disturb that bond once it is in place. Plus, it just makes the boat more palatable to varnish . . .

your tools

Fresh, new single-edged razor blades *and* a razor blade holder
Mineral spirits and clean cotton rags
Citristrip stripping gel (with nitrile gloves, a small chip brush, a cotton terry rag, and a toothbrush)
Te-Ka A&B (with a soft toothbrush and a fresh water supply)

your instructions

1. Carefully scrape off everything that will respond to the razor blade. Take care to use only blades that are fresh and not bent at the blade corners; otherwise, they will scratch unforgivably. Wipe down the surface with mineral spirits when finished.

2. If the surface is fiberglass and some varnish does not respond completely to the razor blade, apply a small amount of Citristrip (see chapter 13) and keep watch until the finish softens, then scrub it off with the toothbrush. (This is your best hope in varnish-encrusted fiberglass nonskid areas.) Wipe off the stripper residue with a wet cloth and rinse clean with fresh water.

3. If teak oil is spilled on your fiberglass, clean it off with a very controlled application of Te-Ka A&B (see chapters 5 and 13 for product information and caveats). Rinse well once all traces of the neutralized Te-Ka have been removed.

. . . and, as you sit home in front of the latest episode of *The Sopranos*, why not do some rubbing out of your own?

how to: *clean the dismantled fittings*

If you have the opportunity, take home all the fittings you tucked into those Ziploc bags (chapter 4) and begin their cleanup. By the time the boat is varnished, they will be spiffed and ready to go back in place, and you won't have spent precious boat time doing this tedious—yet important—work.

the shortcut!

1. Drop the varnish-encrusted fittings into a shallow vat of Citristrip stripping gel. Cover the container.

2. Fuggeddaboudit . . .

3. A few days later, or when you return from the Bahamas with a tan and a rested back, fish the hardware out of the vat (use tongs . . .).

4. Rinse off the shriveled varnish, get out the Liberty Polish (see chapter 13) and replicate the sparkle of your pinkie-ring diamond.

5. If you don't like the looks of the old fasteners, give 'em the heave-ho—*after* paying a little visit to your man at the hardware store.

6. Remember to wear your nitrile gloves for this operation, unless you're trying to remove your fingerprints to confound the Feds.

7. Try to remember which fittings came from which Ziploc bags.

notes

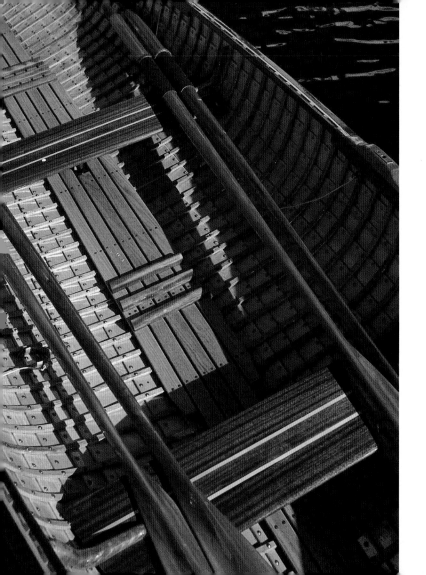

chapter

7

building up to

the grand finale

once the wood is disrobed and sanded to a finish stage there are three treatments that make up *the varnishing prelude*

1. paste wood fillers

2. pigmented stains

3. sealers

You will find no instructions for the first of these treatments in this book. I think paste wood fillers make the wood grain ugly, and I won't be a party to the indolence that underpins their use in lieu of a couple extra buildup varnish coats.

But stains and sealers—these are things I can endorse and, in the case of the latter, submit as a compulsory exercise in one form or another.

how to: *apply stains*

Staining is a step unique to specific woods—most frequently mahogany—and not something one would do as a matter of course in brightwork finishing. Pigmented stains are a standard medium in classic boat restoration and are occasionally cast in the role of problem solver on other boats when troubled wood needs camouflage. Otherwise, this is not a step for universal application.

MATERIALS

Pigmented stain

Poly-Brushes

Mineral spirits

EQUIPMENT

Mason jar with lid

Clean, *lint-free* cotton rags

Stir stick

SAFETY GEAR

Nitrile gloves

Eye shields

optimal weather

Dry, mild

recommended crew

A solo act, but company is nice

attire

F. Maire's painting bibs?

organizing

the boat:
The wood needs to be dry and fine sanded to at least 220 grit, with a hand-sanded final pass to clear away orbital sander swirls (inspect with a swipe of mineral spirits before staining). If fine sanding is completed the day before you plan to stain, cover all work before leaving the boat, to prevent night air and condensation from raising the grain.

the materials and equipment:
Use *fresh* stain, or if using old inventory, make sure no pigment remains stuck to the bottom of the can after shaking. Shake the stain *well*—vigorously, even!—to disperse all pigment, then transfer to a mason jar. Affix a sign to the jar that reads: STIR ME UP! Deposit a stir stick in the jar and leave it there throughout the work.

caveats:
Too many coats of stain will muddy the grain of the wood to the point of looking as though you've painted. Be conservative in the number of coats you apply, unless you're trying to hide something, in which case perhaps you *should* consider painting.

doing the work

1. Test the stain on a small area or piece of trim before applying it to wholesale parts of the boat, to ensure satisfaction with the overall effect.

2. Apply the thoroughly stirred stain with a foam brush in even, successive strokes.

3. As you work, stir often; occasionally put the lid on the jar and give it another good shake. Never let the pigment settle out during the work.

4. Allow the stain to soak into the wood thoroughly but not to the point of drying out. When it is fully absorbed, wipe away any residual stain, and then buff off the excess until the wood sports a uniform shade.

5. Clean spills and drips on surrounding areas and/or hardware *immediately* with a clean cotton rag and mineral spirits.

wrapping up

Allow stain to dry at least 12 to 18 hours before applying the first coat of sealer or varnish. Uncured stain can contaminate the varnish and prevent its drying.

Stain-soaked rags can spontaneously combust while still wet. Take them to your shop or garage and hang them up to dry, then throw them away.

how to: *choose and apply a sealer*

Application of a sealer is the final prevarnish step and offers several opportunities for artistry (plus one very hot issue for debate . . .).

five options for sealing wood
(only three of which I'd recommend . . .)

#1 the commercial sealer: Remember from chapter 3 (about varnish) that a commercially marketed "sealer" is primarily solvent with a bit of oil and resin thrown in, meant to give the wood a thin residual coating after all the solvent has evaporated? None of the varnishes I would recommend calls for the use of such sealing products, and I steer you away from this approach in favor of the next three options.

#2 a wet-sanded coat of tung oil finish: This method of sealing, my *favorite* for sealing teak, nets a richer, far more flattering alternative to paste wood filling, is only slightly more labor intensive, and has commensurate benefits: you achieve earlier leveling of the varnish by filling the grain with a "paste" of the wood's own sanding dust. To seal wood in this fashion, follow the instructions at the end of chapter 8 on applying a tung oil product as a wet-sanded sealer.

#3 the dilute first varnish coat: This is the sealer used almost universally by brightwork refinishers and most often recommended by varnish makers. It is foolproof in its compatibility with the subsequent varnish and is the most convenient because it involves the same materials you already have on hand for the varnish job itself. To seal the wood in this way, follow the instructions in chapter 9 on applying varnish, thinning coat 1 at a ratio of 2 parts varnish to 1 part solvent. Note that the solvent you should always use to do this is the one recommended by the manufacturer for the finishing conditions you find yourself in at that particular time. For cold days, the varnish maker recommends a proprietary thinner that speeds the varnish drying time; that is your thinning solvent for sealing bare wood on that day. For hot days, the varnish maker lists accordingly a companion thinner that will aid brushing, which again constitutes the thinning solvent for sealing the wood under those particular conditions. Do not—I beg you—simply pour in whatever happens to be on your shelf. You risk ruining the varnish and being forced to start from bare wood again. (See chapter 13 for more on varnish and companion solvents.)

#4 the boiled linseed oil soak: This is one of the most beautiful things you could ever do to your mahogany. The grain patterns of African and Honduras mahoganies shimmer like prisms dancing in three-dimensional sunlight when the wood is saturated with oxidized oils and then varnished. *However,* this is not a treatment I'd recommend for the impatient finisher. This process is tedious. The wood can occasionally—when particularly dense—refuse to absorb the oil or dry sufficiently, necessitating some backtracking. But where it works, the effect is well worth the price of the dance.

Read through all the steps first to see whether this sealer is right for your project!

MATERIALS

Boiled linseed oil

Daly's SeaFin teak oil

Japan drier

Poly-Brushes

EQUIPMENT

4-mil plastic sheeting

Coarse cotton shop rags

SAFETY GEAR

Nitrile gloves

optimal weather

Warm and sunny is critical

recommended crew

No incessant talkers

attire

The one time Gucci might be out of place

organizing

the boat: Wood to be fine sanded (to 220) but *not* yet masked for varnishing; lay down 4-mil plastic to catch spills, drips.

the materials and equipment: Mix well 2 parts boiled linseed oil to 1 part Daly's SeaFin teak oil.

caveats: If you attempt this on anything but a dry, warm (78°F at least) day, it won't dry. Wait for the perfect day, start early, and don't get distracted from the coating schedule.

doing the work

1. If it is not a truly HOT day and you are concerned about the oil drying, add a small amount of Japan drier (up to 1 or 2 tablespoons per pint) to the oil mixture.

2. Apply a generous but not sloppy coat of the oil mixture to the wood, using a foam brush.

3. Allow the coat to dry to the touch (this could take anywhere from 15 minutes to 2 hours, depending on the temperature and humidity).

4. When the first coat is dry, apply another coat of the oil mixture. Do not sand between coats.

5. REPEAT the above application until at least six coats have each soaked into the wood and dried.

6. If you have enough warm hours remaining in the day to give you two more working hours, proceed to the last coat; otherwise, save it for the next day.

7. For the final coat, apply the oil and then immediately wet-sand it with 400-grit wet-or-dry paper, taking care not to sand through the finish to bare wood.

8. Buff the sanded oil *before it dries* with shop rags, rubbing delicately in a circular fashion. The dried oil will be very soft, so be gentle!

wrapping up

Let the sealed wood cure at least a day before prepping for varnish. Then, sand lightly with 220-grit paper. If the sanding residue seems to roll up like tiny worms, don't be alarmed; this is normal. Vacuum well, then wipe down the wood with a rag lightly moistened (not soaked) in mineral spirits. Allow the wood to rest a couple hours while you tape and prep the boat for varnish coat 1.

and finally, #5 epoxy sealers . . . Penetrating epoxy sealers have been the subject of much debate and advice-sharing within refinishing circles and over the Internet in the past dozen years. Discussion goes back and forth, round and round: An epoxy sealer creates a perfect foundation for varnish / *It's incompatible and a mistake to use* / It never breaks down / *It's a royal pain to refinish once top coats fail* / It extends the life of the varnish / *It shortens the life of the finisher* / It's cutting-edge material / *It's a gimmick . . .* "Anon Anon Anon . . . ," Mr. Shakespeare might have cried were he cornered with the question.

If you want information on this approach to sealing wood, type the words "penetrating epoxy sealer" into the Internet browser search engine on your computer, and you will find no shortage of cyberwords on the subject. Some people swear by this sealer. I'm still not a believer, despite the seductive theory of it all. But you decide for yourself. If you asked me outright if I would use it, I'd probably answer something like this: Choosing between the three sealing methods recommended above and the one cited here is a little like asking me to choose between a shot of Dalwhinnie and a Rusty Nail. I like my Scotch clean and pure, the way it was designed to be. Once in a while, an ice cube is good. And a twist. Beyond that, I think you wreck the Scotch.

notes

chapter **8**

never

use lard

oiling wood, *for various reasons . . .*

There's a little tale in *Brightwork* that inspires the title of this chapter. I call it the story of the Kansas oil treatment. It's such an amazing *true* story, I think it earns a retelling here.

In our first year in the brightwork business, my sister and I contracted with a Kansas farmer, by phone, to refinish his Ingrid 38, *Kingsblood*. The hull had been trucked from Seattle to the Midwest, where it was finished out, and then trucked back to Seattle for launching and rigging. We were to do the brightwork while it was being rigged, and the plan was to varnish everything except the decks. So on the first day we commenced sanding the toerail to prep the wood. After about an hour of arduous 80-grit work, we were shocked to discover that what we had initially thought was rough, filthy, and blackened ironbark was, in fact, light chestnut *teak*! When the owner finally arrived on the scene later that morning, we asked him what on earth he'd done to such relatively new teak to turn it so black. "Wahll," he started in his shy little Kansas drawl, "the people who built the boat said to put oh'l on the wood, so by golly that's what we did. We put ever' kind of oh'l we could find on it: Crisco oh'l, diesel oh'l, lemon oh'l. We even used lard . . . "

Several lessons were gleaned from that particular boat. This story is plucked from our learning curve and recounted here to shake up the notion that oiling is *ever* a wise thing to do to exterior brightwork. At the very least, it illustrates that even the most rational decision to oil your wood carries with it the imperative to know *which* oils work and which ones turn everything black.

remember yacht refinishing commandment #3:
understand thy chosen finish

This tenet underscores two irrefutable facts about an exterior oil finish:

1. Wood slated for a proper oil finish requires all the same *labor-intensive prep work* called for in varnishing.

2. No oil finish lasts outside, intact, *without monthly refresher coats or a full cover.*

In other words, an exterior oil finish is neither "easier to apply" nor "easier to maintain" than varnish. These are the oiling myths!

how to: *apply an oil finish*

but! an interior oil finish . . .

Now, there's a thing of beauty and a joy forever . . . with the *right* oil, a *wee* bit of work, and a maintenance plan.

Candidates for interior oil finishes: nearly every wood you can name . . . (though some open-grained woods *fare* better varnished—Philippine mahogany, for example).

organizing

the boat: Bring all stripped and/or bleached wood to a fine-sanded stage and do necessary prep detailing on adjacent surfaces, as instructed in previous chapters. Mask around all areas to be finished to prevent scratching of adjacent surfaces (use low-tack tape on painted areas). Lay heavy tarps or 4-mil plastic around work to catch drips. Create proper cross ventilation in work areas, especially below decks.

MATERIALS

1-inch 3M #2040 masking tape

400- and 600-grit 3M Wet-or-Dry sandpaper

Mineral spirits

Daly's SeaFin or comparable quality tung oil formula

Poly-Brushes

Fine bronze wool

EQUIPMENT

Clean cotton shop rags

4-mil plastic sheeting

Sandpaper cutter

Flat rubber sanding blocks

SAFETY GEAR

Nitrile gloves

3M charcoal/dust mask (#9913)

optimal weather

At least 67°F inside the boat

recommended crew

Perfect project for good friends

attire

Flannel is to oiling what fur is to opera

the materials: Cut sandpaper into quarters and fold a few into trifolds; transfer oil to a plastic bottle with a closable top.

caveats:

- You might think you can work carefully enough without masking adjacent surfaces, but don't attempt it. It's very easy to leave hundreds of scratches in your wake during wet-sanding.
- Although oiling seems innocuous, the fumes can be overwhelming. The disposable charcoal masks go a long way in reducing exposure, but proper ventilation cannot be stressed enough.
- Oil-soaked rags can and *do* spontaneously combust; do not leave them in a heap during or after the project. Hang them to dry completely before throwing them out.
- When oiling *veneers*, use *nothing coarser* than 600-grit paper from the beginning.

doing the work

1. Be vigilant, keeping a thinner-moistened rag handy as you work; the oil can seep under masking tape, and undetected runs will haunt you later in dry, shiny form.

2. Set up a plastic-lined paper grocery bag near your work for tossing spent sandpaper as you proceed.

3. Without overloading it, with a foam brush apply the first coat of oil to the prepped wood; allow the oil to soak in completely and dry to the touch.

4. When the wood seems dry (in 70°F air, this should take about 20 minutes), apply another coat and allow it to dry.

5. Apply a third coat to a small section—a size manageable for sanding and rubbing down within the time it takes for oily paste to stay workable.

6. Allow this third coat to soak in for a few minutes, then wet-sand the oil into the wood with 400-grit paper, sanding with the grain, until you produce a tough paste.

7. Make sure you turn the trifold sandpaper surfaces or get new paper often, or you will not produce enough sawdust to create a true paste.

8. When oiling broad, flat surfaces, wrap the sandpaper around a rubber sanding block.

9. Allow paste to sit for 3 to 5 minutes, until just tacky, then buff off in a circular fashion with a clean rag.

10. When buffing, bear down only very lightly, and take care not to extract the paste from beneath the surface and back out of the wood grain itself.

11. Where paste builds up, in corners or around fittings, wrap the rag around a flat, thin surface (a putty knife, for example) and clean away the excess.

12. Give the buffed coat about an hour to dry. Then apply another coat of oil and allow to soak in and dry for about 30 minutes (no longer).

13. Apply a *fifth* coat of oil and repeat the wet-sanding as described above, but—*very important*—use 600-grit paper instead of 400-grit.

14. When the 600-grit residue is very tacky, buff again in a circular fashion to remove excess surface paste. Buff with a clean rag after all the paste is gone.

15. If you want more wood protection (because you have dared to apply this as an *exterior* finish!), apply more penetrating coats between wet-sandings.

16. Linger at the project for at least an hour (supposing a warm environment—longer if colder) after the final buffing for "oil bleed-back patrol."

wrapping up

Before you depart the project, make sure there is no oil bleeding back from the pores of the wood. If you return to find shiny oil specks, you'll need to wet-sand them (with oil) and buff again.

And it cannot be stressed enough: *properly* dispose of rags (hanging them to dry first). Instructions for maintaining an oil finish can be found in chapter 10.

a wet-sanded oil sealer
for application before varnish!

A great way to seal teak before applying the first coat of varnish is to wet-sand a tung oil finish into the bare wood, creating a "self paste wood filler" to level the pores. This is the prettier alternative to commercially packaged paste wood fillers, because the pores blend rather than contrast with the hard meat of the wood. Applying this sealer gives a jump start to the leveling of the varnish, and can reduce the number of varnish coats needed to arrive at a mirror finish. Remember: This is only a sealer, not a finish itself. It must be followed up with varnish.

how to:
apply a wet-sanded oil sealer

Follow all the instructions preceding this for application of an oil finish, using a light tung oil formula (Daly's SeaFin is best—see chapter 13). On all but the softest woods, substitute 360-grit wet-dry sandpaper for the 400-grit paper. Buff carefully, in a circular motion, just enough to remove the surface residue. Then, once the paste is buffed and the wood surface is smooth, allow the wood to sit for 24 hours. Proceed with application of the varnish immediately, thinning the first coat in proportion to the solids content of the varnish (15 percent for Schooner, 25 percent for Epifanes, for example). Do not allow the sealed wood to stand unvarnished or suffer the ravages of the weather, because moisture will cause the filler to swell and raise the grain. This necessitates a repeat wet-sanding of the sealer and another waiting period before the varnish can be applied. Be especially tidy about cleaning oily paste off any fittings and adjacent surfaces; it will look hideous encrusted beneath the new varnish.

chapter

9

the

varnished

truth

Once you have patiently and thoroughly stripped and sanded and prepped and sealed the wood, naught but the zenith of this art remains.

here, then, is

how to varnish . . .

MATERIALS

Your favorite varnish and its companion thinners

Paper buckets—pint size

Cone-style paint strainers

Gerson Super Activated tack cloths

Poly-Brushes, assorted sizes

1-inch 3M Extended Use masking tape

Single-edged razor blades

220- and 320-grit Fre-Cut sandpaper

TOOLS AND EQUIPMENT

Rubber mallet

Ice pick or awl

Clean cotton shop rags

Ziploc bags

Sandpaper cutter

Sanding blocks and sponges

Wet-dry vacuum

SAFETY GEAR

Latex exam gloves

Knee pads

Light-tint UV sunglasses

3M dust masks

optimal weather

Mild and slightly cloudy is *heaven*

recommended crew

Artisans and apprentices

attire

Wear your Sunday varnishing best to please the varnishing gods . . .

organizing

the boat:

After sealing (at least 12 hours later) but before taping for varnish, give the whole boat a bath to eliminate all traces of prep dust and residue. Wipe all brightwork surfaces dry with a clean, lint-free cotton cloth or chamois. Remove all standing water from the boat. If you are varnishing belowdecks, vacuum and wipe down as if prepping for surgery; open hatches at opposite ends of the boat to create proper cross ventilation (to aid drying).

Using 1-inch tape (extended-use for exteriors), mask all surfaces abutting areas to be varnished, pressing firmly along the "varnish edge" of the tape as you go. (Read all there is to know about choosing and using masking tapes in chapter 13.)

the materials and equipment:

Prepare the varnish: pour no more than a cup at a time, along with the manufacturer's recommended solvent, through a strainer into a clean paper bucket, and mix together by gently swirling the varnish in the bucket until the thinner is thoroughly dispersed. Do not stir or shake the varnish to mix, and do *not* varnish straight from the can. See the Standard Coating Schedule (below) for thinning percentages per coat. (See chapter 13 for information about specific varnishes and thinners.)

set up a "movable varnishing station":

When working on the boat: place a cup holding a variety of sizes of clean Poly-Brushes (handles down), along with a fully opened and crumpled tack cloth, the prepped bucket of varnish, a small Ziploc bag for trash, and a supply of chewing gum all in a tidy little flat box that you can scoot along as you work.

caveats:

What you are about to undertake will change your life. It will become an addiction. It will make you crazy. It will make you prideful. You'll never be able to sail your boat again without obsessing over varnish sags and blemishes. Varnish will become what you dream about. It will supplant all other frustrations in your waking hours. It will become the repository for all your angst and longing. Other than that, there's really not much to caution against . . .

doing the work

1. Once the brightwork is wiped down and prepped, a *tack cloth* is your last ticket to a clean, smooth finish. Tack small stretches in front of you *as you work* (3 to 5 feet at a time) and then leave the tack cloth *where you stopped* to remind you to pick it up and continue tacking from there. (Never leave it directly on the warm surfaces of the boat but on a sheet of paper or cardboard, to keep it from leaving a sticky residue in its resting wake.) When tacking, don't *scrub* with the cloth but rather wipe gently over the varnishing plane, just enough to pick up any particulate matter that has settled since the initial wipe-down.

2. For the first three or four coats, apply the varnish in "plaid": Lay the varnish on across the grain, in generous, parallel strokes for several brush widths, then "tip off"—just barely stroking the varnish—without reloading the brush, in the direction of the grain to even out the cross-grain strokes.

3. Work steadily and quickly to avoid losing your wet edge, and monitor the drag of the varnish to determine the need to add brushing thinner.

4. Employ the "roll and tip" tag-team approach when varnishing wide expanses like transoms: one person applies the varnish across the grain in parallel laps with a foam roller while the other immediately tips off the rolled laps, to level the varnish in the direction of the grain. Rolling and tipping is your best hope for a finish free of lap lines and sags, and an efficient way to speed the work on sizable areas.

5. Monitor for holidays and sags as you varnish, and repair these blemishes as you go. Scrape off sags with a razor blade while wet rather than allowing to dry, and quickly feather in a wet patch. (Direct angled lighting is essential to detection of such lapses when varnishing interiors.)

6. If possible, remove any piece that stands vertically and varnish it lying flat. This allows a full depth of varnish per coat and discourages sags.

7. In hot weather, begin with areas that get warmest first, and then follow the shadows around the boat to outsmart the heat. Where there is no escaping the sun, drape light-colored

covers *(free of dust!)* over the prepped brightwork and uncover as you arrive at those spots. If varnishing in spring or fall, beware the invisible morning and afternoon dew, and confine varnishing to the very middle hours of those days. (See What Is a Varnishing Window? later in this chapter.)

8. Apply no more than one coat per day. If your varnish label encourages more than one coat in a day, each is really a solvent-intense half coat.

9. When sanding between coats, sand gingerly at corners and along edges, which hold a much thinner buildup of finish than flat planes.

10. Sand carefully around masking tape, and retape stretches that have become raggedy sources of runs. Remask the entire project after coat 4.

the standard coatings schedule

At the start, you are—presumably—looking at wood sealed in one of the ways recommended in previous chapters. From that stage, the following coatings guide should produce a mirror finish:

COAT 1: Sand sealed wood lightly with 220-grit Fre-Cut paper. (Note: Do not sand after the wet-sanded oil sealer.)

Vacuum; wipe the wood surfaces clean just prior to varnishing with a mineral spirits–moistened rag.

Thin varnish 15 to 25 percent depending on solids content of varnish; allow varnish to dry thoroughly—at least 12 hours.

COAT 2: Sand lightly (220 grit), just enough to see where you're going; vacuum and wipe down with a mineral spirits–moistened rag.

Thin varnish 10 to 15 percent; apply and allow varnish to dry thoroughly—at least 12 hours before sanding for the next coat.

COAT 3: Sand lightly (220 grit), knocking off debris and leaving a moderate scratch; vacuum and wipe down with a mineral spirits–moistened rag.

Thin varnish with one capful of brushing thinner per cup. Apply and allow to dry at least 12 hours.

COAT 4: Sand moderately (220 grit) to start leveling the varnish with the grain; vacuum and wipe down with a mineral spirits–moistened rag.

Thin with only a capful of brushing thinner per cup. Monitor varnish to determine the need to add thinner as you work.

Allow at least 24 hours to dry; the curing time begins to slow with varnish buildup.

COAT 5: Sand in earnest (220 grit) to plane down ridges in pursuit of a mirror plane but taking care not to break through the finish.

Vacuum and wipe down with a mineral spirits–moistened rag. Add a capful of brushing thinner per cup, and more as needed.

Allow at least 24 hours to dry before sanding.

COATS 6–10: The grain "dimples" should gradually be disappearing; sand before each coat (320 grit), vacuum, and wipe down with a mineral spirits–moistened rag. Apply full strength, thinning only to ease brushing. Allow to dry two full days between coats. When all dimples have vanished, and you are looking at a completely glassy surface, you can call it "varnished."

COATS 11+: Apply subsequent "final coats" only in pursuit of perfection, if for some reason you are not content with what you have.

BEYOND 15 COATS: You need professional help . . . and I don't mean *me*.

which thinner to use? The thinners called out in the coatings schedule are governed by the application conditions on the day you apply the varnish. The label on the varnish typically refers to that company's recommended thinners. For cold days, use the thinner specified for spraying. Most companies package a proprietary can of steam-distilled mineral spirits for brushing in warm weather.

what is a varnishing window? It is that stretch of daylight when one has any business applying varnish. Its configuration within the varnishing day stretches and shrinks with the seasons and according to one's latitude. If you varnish at noon in a Los Angeles July, you'll be thinning to the point of insanity. If you varnish at 4 p.m. in a Seattle September, you'll return to a dried coat that is *opaque*. The mere presence of sunshine does not imply a varnishing opportunity. Become familiar with the readings of the thermometer and the barometer. They *each* constrain the varnishing window. (Of course, common sense is a handy guide, too.)

what is a holiday? This is the classic term for a "skip" in your varnishing. Isn't it perfect?

It is also what you may take, once all your hard work is completed.

wrapping up

Once the final coat is cured and the tape has been carefully removed, begin the reassembling process. Detail the boat: take a razor blade or some Citristrip to any runs and varnish messes (on fiberglass). Spot-clean oil spills with Te-Ka A&B where appropriate. Install *clean* hardware, using new fasteners (see preparatory detailing in chapter 6). Go easy with a power screwdriver around fresh varnish. Don't overtighten screws.

Ten new coats of varnish will require about six months to season before the finish is really cured. Be gentle with the finish during this period.

When the boat is all back together and looking ready for the prom, have a celebration! Uncork a beautiful bottle of champagne and toast your place in the noble varnishing legacy passed down through the ages. Congratulations!

notes

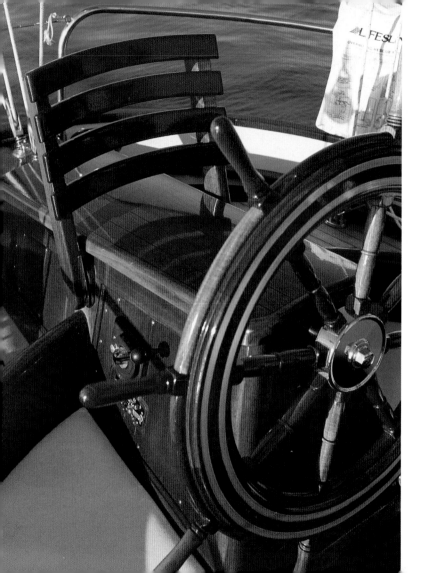

now,

let's try to keep

it that way,

soldier

setting up and KEEPING the maintenance program

Bearing in mind the sad tale introducing chapter 2, here are a few pointers for *keeping* your brightwork beautiful, thus increasing the odds that the two happiest days in your life with your boat will *not* be the day you bought it and the day you sold it.

varnish cleaning . . .

Give the brightwork a regular rinse-off: a freshwater hosing, wiped dry with soft, clean cloths or a chamois.

If soap is called for, use something mild like Murphy Oil Soap; swab gently and rinse thoroughly afterward.

Don't leave salt water to dry on your varnish. The dried crystals act like millions of tiny heat guns, speeding the departure of the varnish and, worse, feel like sandpaper grit when rubbed along and into the finish.

. . . and preventive maintenance

Don't subject varnish to great tests of abrasion: run mooring lines sensibly; and keep grit and salt water hosed off.

Wipe off the dew—gently—with a clean chamois first thing each morning when cruising.

Adopt a "SHOES OFF THE VARNISH" rule; forbid guests from planting fannies with riveted pockets on the brightwork.

I repeat: invest in the Brightwork Insurance and Retirement Plan—*canvas covers*. They pay for themselves, over and over.

refresher varnish coats . . .

Plan "refresher coats" in advance, not at the first sign of deterioration or dulling of the finish. Two-coat refreshers, twice a year, are optimum. (Once the boat is taped for the work, it's silly not to apply a second coat.) Over the life of a healthy finish, this might seem like a regimen that could net an obscene buildup of varnish, but in fact it does not. Aside from the natural shrinkage that takes place as the varnish foundation ages, the prep and between-coat sanding done every year reduce the depth of the finish to balance the addition of new coats. In essence, what you end up refinishing each year are the same top coats, taking off the old and putting on the new.

Here's the drill for application of REFRESHER coats:

1. Wash the whole boat, using a mild soap (see chapter 13) and fresh water; rinse well. Then wipe down all the brightwork with a mixture of 1 part water and 3 parts denatured alcohol. This cuts cleanly through residue that might prevent adhesion of the new varnish.

2. Remove "easy fittings"; sand brightwork moderately (320 grit); vacuum and wipe down with a mineral spirits–moistened rag. Mask with 1-inch tape (extended-use tape is best if you're leaving it on more than two days).

3. Apply the varnish (the same product used originally); allow it to dry at least twenty-four hours before prepping for the next coat.

4. Repeat steps 2 and 3 for a second coat; remove tape and reassemble fittings.

. . . and varnish repairs
("Scratch and Patch")

Varnish dings and cracks can be "bandaged" between—or in preparation for—refresher coats, to extend the life of an otherwise honorable finish. This is what we call Scratch and Patch work. If you perform this work throughout the year, especially as a periodic ritual during cruises, herculean labors are avoided later, when you return to port or at refresher coat time.

- The minute you notice a broken varnish seal at an otherwise healthy joint, or if a brightwork trim suffers a sudden scrape, mask precisely along that joint or abraded area and reseal with varnish (see Pack a Brightwork First-Aid Kit later in this chapter).

- If the finish has lifted at a joint—evidenced by a yellowish "blister"—scrape the blister away carefully up to where it meets the adhered finish, using a very sharp hook scraper. Try to scrape off no more than the lifted varnish itself.
- If the wood appears darkened once the blistered varnish is removed, bleach the area carefully using Teak Wonder (see chapter 13) and a soft nylon scrubber or soft toothbrush, resisting the temptation to scrub out the pith of the grain. Rinse thoroughly and allow the wood to dry completely.
- If there is a chance the joint is holding water, extract all water with a wet-dry vacuum, then allow the area to air out for at least one warm day until absolutely dry. Do not revarnish until you are certain all moisture is eliminated from the joint.
- Once the wood is dry, sand just enough to remove the raised fuzz from the wood (120, then 220 grit).
- Stain and/or seal the area as you did for the original finish.
- Make a "jet speed" version of your varnish, diluting it 25 percent with its companion fast-drying solvent (the one recommended by the manufacturer for spraying the varnish). Apply this varnish and allow 4 hours to dry.
- Without sanding between coats, apply a second coat of varnish, thinned 15 percent with the same solvent.
- Build up the patch with subsequent full-strength coats, a day apart, sanding between each coat to fair the patch.
- When the patch is level with the good finish, lightly sand (320 grit) the whole piece to fair the patch, then apply a full coat of varnish.

is this finish good enough to simply refresh?

Or do I need to strip and start from bare wood? The only answer is a question back:

Will the refresher coat have more integrity than the finish beneath it? If "No," refresh. If "Yes," strip 'er down!

maintaining an oil finish

Applying maintenance coats to properly oiled wood (see chapter 8) is the easiest part of that finish. You just have to be prepared to do it *every month* if you've gone that route on *exterior* brightwork. For interiors, once every other *year* is a fine maintenance regimen. Annual refresher coats are typically necessary only in high-wear areas, like around the galley or companionway or on frequently handled trims. Along with losing their finish, these spots get grimy, and a pass with bronze wool and oil is an excellent way to clean off the scurf.

1. Use extra-fine bronze wool *(never steel wool!)* instead of foam brushes and wet-or-dry sandpaper to apply the oil.

2. Work the oil into the wood, in the direction of the grain, then allow it to sit a few minutes until tacky.

3. Buff the surface clear with a dry, clean cotton shop rag.

4. Repeat until wood is clean and no longer finish starved.

5. Bleed-back should be minimal, but linger awhile when finished just to make sure you catch any emerging glossy freckles.

pack a brightwork first-aid kit!

Your brightwork is finished, and you *finally* get to push away from the dock and go cruising. Take a little emergency varnishing kit along for the inevitable dings and scrapes. When trauma hits, you can administer a temporary patch (for once, it's OK to varnish straight from the can . . .). That way, you keep moisture out of the wood and the surrounding finish intact until more serious repair work can take place back at port.

In a hard plastic Multi-File (available at office supply outlets), here is what I've packed for clients:

1 pint varnish (Interlux Schooner)
6 each: 1- and 2-inch Poly-Brushes
1 Gerson tack cloth in a Ziploc bag

2 sheets each: 80-, 120-, 220-grit Fre-Cut sandpaper,
  quartered, in a Ziploc bag
4 clean rolled-up cotton shop rags or baby diapers
1 pint steam-distilled mineral spirits (Interlux #333)
1 roll 3M #2040 1-inch masking tape in a Ziploc bag
Single-edged razor blades—5-pack box
A sharpened 1-inch Red Devil hook scraper in a Ziploc bag
A paint-can opener

11

cabin

soles, decks, and

spars. oh my!

three special brightwork challenges

In the world of yacht refinishing, design details can vary from one trim or bulwark or toerail to the next. We run into the occasional *dreaded* louvered companionway door or the daunting butterfly hatch. We find ourselves working on mahogany or teak or ironbark or a host of other exotic woods. In short, differences in brightwork subject abound. But the majority of projects share a common theme:

You strip, you sand, you prep, you apply the finish.

You head off to sea.

More or less . . .

Then there are the exceptions.

cabin soles, decks, and spars . . .
each throws into our pathway a distinct set of finishing hurdles

These projects can force us into physical and emotional contortions that seem beyond the human pale.

They conspire with Mother Nature to make us insane. They inspire fantasies of large bonfires.

They have the power to break us.

Still, their will must be done. Here's a little order to impose in the execution of these particular tasks.

cabin soles . . .

In the good old days, cabin soles were constructed of teak planks, separated by holly strips that stuck up proud to provide sure footing during adverse sailing conditions. They were designed for function, and nobody fussed too much over their finish. Today, the teak and holly "look," though still the classic cabin sole, is fashioned from plywood boards that sport but a thin membrane of hardwood at the surface. These veneers, albeit charming to look at, lose their countenance in a hurry if not well protected from day one.

standing up . . . or on your knees?

The first order of cabin sole business has nothing to do with the finish itself but how your body will commune with the project . . .

Some cabin soles come out of the boat *in toto,* at the turn of several screws. Swans win the "best cabin soles" prize with me for this feature. These soles, and others like them, are best varnished atop a stable of sawhorses in your garage or back at the shop. The final finish not only looks nicer, you and your spine will be sitting pretty, too.

Other cabin soles are not as kind. They must be finished in "scullery maid position" because they don't come out. Your back will hurt, and the varnish fumes can make you woozy. It's a nasty job. But if the sole needs to be refinished, you can't ignore it; otherwise, you end up looking down at plywood substrates in no time. Just be smart about the finish you use, then carry the memory of the job into the way you treat the cabin sole once it's finished.

what IS this finish?

Many boats, especially ones from Asian boatbuilders, come with epoxy-type finishes on the cabin sole. While the tenacious prom-ise of these finishes helps to sell boats, the finish on some boards invariably starts breaking down at edges and in high-traffic areas. Matching or even stripping these finishes can be difficult if not downright impossible by traditional means. If your attempts with the heat gun fail, and a patient application of Citristrip (allowing ample time for it to soften) does not give you results, you may need to resort to methylene chloride strippers to remove such a finish, and then consult the manufacturer for directions if you wish to match the finish originally used.

tips for finishing cabin sole boards
at the shop

removing the cabin sole: Make a map: As each board is pulled up, write a number on the back corresponding to its place on the map. Use a waterproof marker. Also mark a B at the edge that points to the bow. Label each pull-ring to match its board number, and place the hardware in a Ziploc bag along with the screws.

stripping/bleaching the boards: If the old finish is an oil, it can be bleached off using Te-Ka A&B. The key: apply each part of the formula using *only* a cellulose sponge, not bristles or nylon pads. Rinse carefully and squeegee water off to speed drying time and minimize the risk of raising or delaminating the veneer.

If the old finish is varnish, remove it with a heat gun. If a little varnish still clings to the pores, determine whether it makes more sense to strip the remainder using Citristrip or just lightly sand to knock off the last of the old finish. Take great care not to gouge or overheat the veneer with the scraper and heat gun, and not to sand through the veneer if wrapping up the stripping with sandpaper (use only 150 grit or *finer*).

If the varnish is broken down in areas but the majority of the finish is still intact, lightly bleach discolored spots as directed above *before* doing any heat-gun stripping. Then, once those bleached areas are lightly sanded, build up the finish in increments before varnishing the full boards.

For sanding and varnishing directions, proceed to Tips for Finishing a Cabin Sole Regardless of Location later in this chapter, factoring in these additional details:

1. Mask carefully around the edges of each board at the beginning of varnish work, and remask halfway through the coat-ings schedule. Pull the tape and varnish the edges as you apply the final two coats.

2. Even if working alone, *roll and tip* (see Doing the Work, rolling and tipping, in chapter 9) to apply the varnish. The varnish will build up more evenly and quickly this way than if applied by brush alone.

tips for finishing a cabin sole
in place

If only a few of the boards are removable, leave the entire sole in place. The finish will build up more consistently across all the boards, and you won't be fighting the "battle of the bilge" trying to keep from falling through the open spots as you finish the fixed portions of the sole.

If the "in-place" cabin sole needs bleaching . . . do not use Te-Ka A&B, because there's no way to properly rinse away the dregs (without sinking the boat . . .)

Use instead Daly's A&B Bleach (see chapter 13).

This is a two-part hydrogen peroxide product. The parts are *mixed together* to create a bleach strength appropriate to your needs.

1. In a Pyrex container, mix the bleach in equal parts for average bleaching; add additional B to heighten bleaching strength.

2. Wearing nitrile gloves, lightly scrub the sole with the bleach mixture, using a soft nylon pad.

3. As you complete each area, thoroughly wipe up the filthy dregs with cotton rags. Do this cleaning over the entire sole.

4. Starting over, and using a wide Poly-Brush, "paint" a fresh coat of the bleaching solution on the entire sole; allow to dry overnight.

5. Once dried, wipe off the crystallized bleach with cotton rags and a solution of 2 parts water to 1 part denatured alcohol.

6. Allow the cabin sole to dry for 24 hours before sanding.

For sanding and varnishing directions, proceed to Tips for Finishing a Cabin Sole Regardless of Location (next section), factoring in these additional details:

- Mask precisely over the pull-ring hardware on the hatch boards, leaving rings in the UP position for pulling boards during the project.
- Once the sole is sanded, pull the hatch boards, sand the outside edges of the boards *and* the inside edges of abutting perimeters, and mask both sets of edges carefully. Put the boards back into place and varnish the sole with the boards in place. Pull and replace the edge taping after the third and sixth coats; after the eighth coat, pull off the tape and varnish all the edges. Do not apply more than two coats to either of the edges, or the hatch boards will stick when, in the future, you want to pull them out.
- After each sanding, including sanding between varnish coats, vacuum the entire boat (not just the cabin sole), and then wipe down all surfaces with a moist cotton cloth. To minimize stirring up dust *during* vacuuming, it's nice to have an extra-long hose made for your wet-dry canister vacuum (consult a local hose supply company for this) and leave the canister, with its exhaust outlet blasting away, *outside* the boat while vacuuming. Set up a box fan in the companionway to help *draw* dusty air out of the boat as you vacuum. This minimizes the amount

of dust that will settle back down and into the varnish.

- During the varnishing, open several ports or an opposite hatch overhead, and set up the companionway fan again; run it on its lowest speed. This pulls fumes out of the boat and increases air circulation, which aids drying of the finish.
- Wear a 3M disposable charcoal mask (see chapter 13) when varnishing interiors, especially when using Interlux #60 Rubbed Effect varnish.

tips for finishing a cabin sole
regardless of location

sanding the veneer sole to prepare for varnish: If the sole is relatively new veneer, you may use an orbital sander, but *only* with 320-grit or *finer* paper. Test sanding grits on the least conspicuously located board, starting with the finest grit and working backwards through the grits, to determine which fairs the surface most efficiently without mowing through the veneer. If at *all* doubtful about the depth of the veneer, err on the side of more labor-intensive hand-sanding, using nothing coarser than 220 grit wrapped around a cork block.

varnishing the cabin sole: Refer to Doing the Work in chapter 9 for general varnishing directions, and apply appropriate points to the project at hand.

Seal bare wood with a dilute coat of your varnish. Apply no fewer than eight coats of varnish, including the sealer coat. Sand between all coats.

The best varnish for a satin cabin sole finish is Interlux #60 Goldspar Satin (see chapter 13). But a tip: for the first six coats, varnish with a high-abrasion gloss varnish (Interlux Clipper Clear, for example—see chapter 13), then use the satin varnish for the final two or three coats. This nets a more tenacious sole *and* prevents the wood from losing its clarity from too many coats of pigmented varnish.

a tip for a newly built cabin sole: If you have the luxury of starting out with a new boat with an unfinished cabin sole, the job is half done. Protect that "labor-saved" asset by taping down a full-floor cardboard cover for the commissioning phase of the boat, and leave the cardboard down until the very day you intend to begin finishing the sole. (Even if the sole on your new boat is finished, this is a smart way to keep the sins of the commissioning crew from becoming a permanent fact of the sole.) Prep a new bare veneer sole by sanding with 320 grit, carefully with an orbital sander, or by hand.

if the cabin sole is made of solid planks: it will likely be teak, in which case there are several finishing options: the varnish finish described above, an oil finish (see chapter 8 for instructions on applying an oil finish), or a bare, foot-worn patina. Whatever befits the character of the boat will suit the needs of the sole. You have only to choose.

taking care of your new cabin sole finish

Give a newly varnished cabin sole at least one full week to cure before walking on it. Two is even better. Impose a "no-shoes" policy for the first month while the varnish cures completely.

Refresh the finish when it starts looking scratched or battered; don't wait for it to start peeling. Repair damaged spots or high-wear areas as soon as possible, but at least once between cruising seasons. Full refreshers would be appropriate every two or three years, depending on the way the boat is used. Refresh with the same varnish used for top coats, prepping with a wipe of 2 parts water to 1 part denatured alcohol and 320-grit sanding.

Apply full refreshers in fall or spring, but try to avoid this project in other seasons. It will severely limit cruising time if done in summer. And winter poses too many climatic challenges for drying varnish and safe application.

teak decks ... *a short rant, by yours truly*

A teak deck is the most *misunderstood* chunk of wood on a boat. People are constantly confusing it with a piece of furniture.

It is not a Chippendale sideboard. It is just a floor! And it is *not* the 200-year-old pumpkin pine–planked floor in Martha Stewart's library. It is just a simple, innocent teak floor—a floor meant to do battle with the sea.

However, in its simplicity it is a noble floor, fashioned from a noble, self-sufficient wood.

It is built to stand *naked* before the world, without shame, without the false flattery of men, without the dubious protection of manufactured "dressings."

It is Eve before the serpent's arrival.

It can greet Mother Nature *and* Martha Stewart face to face, sure of foot come hell or high water.

Leave it alone already! Quit insulting it with all those charlatan sealers.

Quit feeding your brown wood predilections by slathering oil from stem to stern.

Quit assaulting it with Spic 'n Span and bristle brushes.

And, for the love of God, lose the Ajax cleanser!

Wise up! Treat it with respect!

Then afford it some intelligent neglect.

Treat it like a TEAK DECK
or be forever condemned to the labors that follow ...

how to treat a teak deck ...

The most beautiful teak deck I've ever known was on a southern California Swan named *Pristine*. Here's how *Pristine*'s owners treated her decks:

- Regular swabbings with a *cellulose sponge mop* and a bucket of mild soapy water
- Regular dousings with buckets of clear salt water whenever out sailing

That's it. No sealers, no nonsense, no sweat.

With that regimen, the decks turned as silver as a December moon, and remained as smooth and solid as the day they were built, year after year.

symptoms of a healthy deck

- Completely flat grained, fair and smooth at the surface
- Naturally light brown if freshly built or if freshly bleached and sanded
- Light silver from oxidation of natural surface oils after 6+ months' exposure to sun
- Not black or dark gray from unchecked mildewing
- No applied oil, silicone, or other "sealer" coatings
- No shrunken deck seams or voids and gaps in the caulking
- No exposed fasteners or missing bungs

If your deck is lucky enough to be in this wonderful condition, you can *keep it that way indefinitely* with the following approach:

the pristine deck maintenance program

- A "weekly washdown" using fresh water and a small amount of Lemon Joy or Shaklee's Basic I
- A periodic soaking with clean salt water, or fresh water to which you've added ⅛ cup TSP (trisodium phosphate) per gallon
- A "SPONGES ONLY, NO BRISTLES OF ANY KIND, NO EXCEPTIONS, NO MERCY FOR OFFENDERS" deck-cleaning policy
- *A full boat cover* (also known as Deck Insurance) if regular washdowns are not logistically feasible

If your decks are currently in a calamitous state, it's too early (or too late?) to be planning proper care and maintenance.

Don't despair! A healthy deck is a few laborious steps down the road . . . *then* you can mend your ways and implement proper care . . .

the teak deck myths!

A simple caretaking program escalates into A Major Retrieval Project all too often through misunderstanding of the realities of teak deck ownership and naïveté about the wood itself. Do your deck a favor and disabuse yourself of the following notions:

MYTH	REALITY
My teak deck needs to be "sealed" to hold up. (Someone told me the wood could split without a sealer.)	Sealers: *all faux, no friend.* . . . (The teak is already sealed *from within*, by its *own* superior oils!)
My deck is prettier when it's oiled and brown. (Plus, movie stars' boats always have brown decks. . . .)	If ya' gotta have brown decks, get a boat with a brown gelcoated deck. (Besides, movie stars have a full-time staff doing deck maintenance.)
The teak won't come clean without stiff brushes. (It's the only way to dig all that black gish out of the grain!)	The day you introduced bristles to the deck, you *ruined* the grain. . . . (Bristle brushes are what *open* up the grain for "gishy" mildew to grow.)
Doesn't excavated grain provide better footing? (Though I *do hate* that it turns so black all the time. . . .)	Healthy *flat* teak is a natural nonskid, which is why boatbuilders use it! (And with bristle scrubbing, millions of little troughs form in the grain, where water sits, turning the teak black with mildew again within weeks.)
Power-washing services are the modern way! (The deck is brand spanking clean in *no* time! Look, Ma, no kneeling!)	Power-washing your teak deck is like sandblasting your face. . . . (Just like your deck, the screws will be showing in no time. Look Ma, no wood left!)

how to: *rescue mildewed decks that have been oiled*

To remove an oil-gone-bad finish from your deck, you will need the brute force of Te-Ka A&B. For instructions on bleaching with this product, turn to How to Bleach Off a Finish in chapter 5 and follow *all* the directives there, paying close attention to the admonitions about personal safety. Be aware of one great caveat, however: if your topsides are painted, Te-Ka A&B will damage the paint unless you install a bulletproof bleaching skirt. (You might be safer with the product that follows, for cleaning up the mildewed surface, and then sanding heavily to remove any residual oil finish.)

When the decks are bleached and have had a day to dry, proceed to How to Sand Decks later in this chapter.

how to: *rescue decks that are black with mildew but not oiled*

Decks that have *not* been adulterated in any way but suffer from long-term neglect and exposure to moisture can appear hopelessly black and ugly. Fear not! There *is* hope, in the form of another bleaching regimen called Teak Wonder Cleaner and Brightener (see chapter 13).

Before you tackle this project, determine whether the grain is so thoroughly excavated from years of bristle cleaning that you might not be ahead of the game doing the heavy-grit sanding first (50 grit on a half-sheet orbital; do *not* use a belt sander . . .). Do this *before* bleaching, sanding just enough to remove the bulk of the ridges. This is wood you know you'll have to sacrifice anyway in the interest of planing the decks flat. Taking this approach will save you dollars in materials, because you won't be using Teak Wonder on wood that is essentially meant to be lopped off.

To bleach with Teak Wonder, refer to materials and boat setup lists and Doing the Work instructions for Te-Ka bleaching in chapter 5, along with the Doing the Work instructions here, factoring in these additional details:

- The Teak Wonder label gives the impression that using the brightener is optional. It is *not*, so do not be tempted to skip that step.
- This product is murder on anodized aluminum. Protect any aluminum trims by either removing them from the boat altogether, covering them tightly with duct tape and plastic, or coating them with a thick layer of carnauba wax (taking care not to slop wax over onto the wood). When bleaching is finished, buff off the wax, and you'll have shiny, unscathed aluminum.
- Unlike Te-Ka A&B, with Teak Wonder you do the entire boat with the teak cleaner first; then when the cleaning residue is rinsed off the boat, you go back and brighten all the wood, halting the detergent action of the cleaner with the application of a citric acid solution.
- Read and follow directions on the Teak Wonder label, but ignore the invitation to apply the Teak Wonder sealer once the wood is dry.

doing the work

1. Start at the highest point on the boat and work down.

2. Rinse the entire boat, and thoroughly soak the deck before beginning work.

3. Shake the bottle labeled Teak Cleaner well, then apply generously and evenly, spreading with the aid of a *soft* tile scrubber.

4. Allow the cleaner to penetrate the wet wood for a couple of minutes, then scrub lightly in a circular motion until the solution lathers up.

5. Allow the froth to sit while you move on to another section and repeat all the above.

6. Alternate between sections, whipping the cleaner on each into a lather back and forth for a total of three times, adding a little more cleaner wherever needed.

7. Do not rush to rinse the lathered areas, even after the third frothing. Allow them to sit as long as they can remain moist.

8. If it's warm, keep the lather moist by sending a fine spray mist over the scrubbed areas before each new frothing.

9. When finished with an entire section (the whole port side, for example), rinse the area until all the foam is clear.

10. Dislodge any gunk from nooks and crannies by gently nudging with a soft toothbrush, resisting the temptation to scrub the wood firmly.

11. To hasten the departure of the dirty foam, run the tile scrubber over the wood as you rinse.

12. If you employ a spray nozzle, use it on the shower, not the power spray, setting, or you risk excavation of the softened pith of the grain.

13. Once all sections of the deck are bleached and rinsed, go back and give the entire boat another thorough rinse.

14. After the decks have drained but before they begin to dry, apply the brightener, a section at a time, spreading with a huge cellulose sponge.

15. As each section is restored to a bright golden hue (this happens fairly quickly), rinse it off. Move on to brighten the next section accordingly.

16. If, when all is brightened, you notice any spots that have bled back or are considerably darker than others, reapply brightener and allow to sit.

17. When all brightening work is complete, rinse the entire boat again, using the power spray nozzle but going at it gently.

18. Rinse until you've made three complete passes over the boat.

19. When finished for the day, don't forget to inspect belowdecks for any leaks; wipe up any water that has found its way inside the boat.

20. Allow the wood to dry completely before sanding.

how to: *sand decks once they've been bleached*

Bleaching, regardless of which system you've used, raises the wood grain. Even with efforts to scrub gently, the surface becomes fuzzy and some of the pith gets pulled from the grain. If you waltz off after the last round of rinsing and call it good, although it might *seem* that the work is behind you, trouble will follow, and sooner than you expect. Rain and dirt will collect in those little valleys and pores, and mildew will come riding back into town on a very fast horse. Sanding the grain back to flush gives the wood a more efficient runoff surface, thereby preventing excess moisture from lingering on the decks and inviting the growth of mildew.

Even if you've elected to mow down big ridges *before* the bleaching, the resultant fuzz raised by the big bath necessitates a "finishing-grit pass" to complete the project. Roll up your sleeves and get out your sanders.

how soon should I sand?

Sand as soon as possible after bleaching once the decks have dried at least a day. If brightwork trims are slated for varnish work, you can save the deck sanding for last, to clean up any "accidents," but I think it's nice to get this grubby sanding project out of the way *before* the varnishing. It makes for a more pleasant work site, and if you save it until last, all that heavy sanding grit flying around can dull the gloss of a new varnish job. If you're worried about varnish drops finding their way onto the freshly sanded decks, tape cardboard over the decks for the duration of the varnish work, or use good, *clean* drop cloths as you brush.

the pesky protruding deck seam

is an occasional impediment in deck sanding. If the seam caulking on your deck has squeezed up proud of the teak, sanding the decks will take twice as long. Circumvent this problem: trim those seams *before* you begin sanding.

- **Your tool:** Single-edged razor blades (buy by the 100 if trimming an entire deck)
- **Your "raw to the bone" defense:** Band-Aids or masking tape, wrapped *in advance* around the first two joints of *both* index fingers
- **Your attack:** Bend the razor blade just slightly in the center to create a gentle arc. Then, holding at both sides and starting at one end of a seam, sslide the concave blade under the caulking—pulling toward you, keeping the blade steady and

flush with the wood as you go. CAUTION: Avoid gouging the wood!

As you work, replace your blade at the first sign of dulling. Vacuum up slivers of caulking as you go, and dispose of long stretches that accrue. On a big deck, this can feel like an interminable task. Enlist the help of good buddies and share old college stories as you work. Award a prize for the longest cut!

now may I finally sand?

Now you may finally sand. As you plan the project, refer to chapter 6 for details about sanding in general, as well as chapters 12 and 13 for information about sanders and sanding aids, sandpaper, and masking tapes to be used in this project. Add to all that these additional details specific to the task at hand:

- *Do not* use disc or belt sanders on your deck. The Porter-Cable half-sheet finishing sander is best for this job. It's heavy, powerful, and *flat.*

- If you can't get your hands on the half-sheet sander, use Porter Cable Speed-Bloc orbitals and increase the workforce.
- To determine the grit of sandpaper needed, buy a sheet each of 50-grit 3M Production paper and 60-, 80-, and 120-grit Fre-Cut, and test them all.
- For *extremely* open-grained wood, ridges come down quickest with 50-grit 3M Production paper; otherwise, do heavy fairing work with 60 grit.
- If starting with 50 grit, plan a two-phase follow-up: 80 grit to cut out the 50-grit scars, and 120 grit to clarify the grain and smooth the surface.
- If starting with 60 grit, do the clarifying and smoothing work with 120 grit. If you're having the time of your life, add a 180-grit beauty phase!
- Buy at least a *sleeve* of heavy-grit paper for the average 40-foot teak deck. Buy a sleeve of 120 grit, and use the extra paper for later work.
- Do not attempt this job alone. Your back will never forgive you.

TOOLS AND EQUIPMENT

Porter-Cable Speed-Bloc quarter- and half-sheet orbital finishing sanders

Wet-dry vacuum with brush nozzle and crevice tool attachments

Counter brush or whisk broom

Sandpaper cutter

Assorted hand-sanding aids

Screwdrivers and/or VSR driver/drill and bits

50-foot extension cord (one per sander) and a source of electrical power

Single-edged razor blades (for seams)

MATERIALS

1- and 2-inch 3M #2040 masking tape

Appropriate sandpaper—heavy and finishing grits

Clean cotton shop rags or chamois

Ziploc bags

Large paper grocery bags

SAFETY GEAR

Nitrile gloves

3M particulate respirator

optimal weather

Moderately warm; *dry, no rain!*

recommended crew

A time to call in all outstanding favors . . .

attire

Dress for comfort and speed, my dear; this is no time for vanity . . .

organizing

the boat: Lock down all hatches and ports; stuff rags into the Dorades. *Double-mask* along all surfaces slated for sanding (one strip atop another). Remove all items that reside on the decks. Remove any nonbedded fittings (and place them, with fasteners, in a Ziploc bag) and double-tape around ones that cannot be removed.

the materials and equipment: Cut up as much paper as you think you'll need for several hours, for sanders and hand-sanding; organize the vacuum, sanders, cords, sandpaper, and trash receptacles in a central spot where they won't need to be disturbed during the work.

caveats: If you're the religious sort, this job can destabilize your faith. It is mind-numbingly exhausting, especially when decks are in horrible shape to begin with. Enlist some help; start early; drink Gatorade—*not beer*—until the day is done. Most important: be *extremely* vigilant about the risk of scratching adjacent surfaces with the heavy-grit paper.

doing the work

1. Start by machine at one end of the boat and work your way to the other, keeping the storm of sawdust brushed aside as you proceed.

2. Vacuum periodically to keep the gritty dust from clogging the sandpaper, and to keep a clear visual path of work ahead.

3. Drag a cuffed paper grocery bag alongside as you work, and discard spent sandpaper there rather than adding to the mess on the boat.

4. When all machine-sanding is completed, go back and hand-sand areas too tight for the sanders.

5. Once finished with heavy grit by both machine and hand, start over with the finishing-grit paper by machine.

6. Proceed exactly as with heavy-grit paper, following up with hand-sanding at the end of the machine work.

7. If you are unable to complete all the work the first day, vacuum

up the accumulated dust, pull the masking tape, and remask the next day.

8. If you *do* finish the job in one day, pull the tape, vacuum thoroughly, and clear away all the work equipment from the decks.

9. Get out your hose, attach the spray nozzle, and give the *entire* boat—including covers, lines, spars, and topsides—a thorough shower.

10. Flush grit and dust from every nook and cranny until you can't stand another minute with the hose.

11. Wipe any brightwork dry with a chamois or soft, clean cotton cloths.

12. Allow the decks to drain well before setting resident paraphernalia back in place.

13. If fittings require bedding compound, install those on another day, after the teak has dried completely.

and spars . . . oh my!

Keep a watchful eye on that finish on your mast. Trouble starts quietly beneath and spreads insidiously . . .

varnish your mast every year!

There are two positions from which to refinish a bright spar

1. unstepped: If the finish is even slightly on its way toward failing, pull the stick and finish it prone.

2. from the chair: Annual refreshers can be done inexpensively and quickly from the bosun's chair.

schedule an annual inspection ride in the bosun's chair:

- to determine levels of finish deterioration and overall condition of the stick
- to determine the position from which you will need to do annual varnish work

    Do *not* wait until the day you plan to work to go up and *find out* what shape the mast is in. Murphy's Law will be invoked and precious time will disappear down the drain of poor planning.

The following tips for finishing spars, both unstepped and from the chair, *supplement* prep and varnishing guidelines found in earlier chapters.

varnishing an unstepped mast

preparing the mast

- Set up the mast on at least four strong, well-engineered sawhorses.
- Remove all hardware. Remove the track and clean off all crusty buildup and old bedding compound to make ready for later reinstallation.
- Plan to rotate the mast for stripping, bleaching, and sanding. Keep thick layers of clean rags under the mast at the sawhorses, cushioning the wood throughout the prep phases.

stripping

- On round spars, chemical stripping—though messy and more expensive in materials costs—goes quickest. Just make sure you lay a "floor" of 4-mil plastic sheeting under the work, to contain the gooey fallout.

The Key: apply only *one* coat of Citristrip; allow to sit for about ten minutes, then scrape off quickly with the grain, with a sharp hook scraper, taking care not to rip into the wood itself. *Rinse thoroughly.*

- On square spars, stripping with a heat gun is best, because the flat planes give up more finish on each scrape. And once you own a heat gun, there's little point in pouring dollars down the stripper drain.

The Key: teamwork! One person heats, the other comes directly along with the scraper.

bleaching

- *Before* bleaching, do the heavy-grit sanding (see Sanding, next column).
- If moisture stains are deeply set, follow guidelines for bleaching with oxalic acid (chapter 6). Use the paste method, allowing the bleach to sit overnight.
- If stains are superficial, bleach with Te-Ka A&B.

- Any stains that remain past bleaching become part of the patina of the mast. Accept their presence, resisting the urge to scrub or sand heavily. However, be vigilant for signs of future rot in *all* "bruised" areas.

sanding

- The heavy-grit sanding (60 to 80 grit) determines the whole look of the spar. When doing this work, imagine you are Michelangelo sculpting the *Pietà*.
- On round spars, when doing heavy-grit work, use an orbital finishing sander, and work like a lathe. Sand round and round, albeit across the grain, to maintain the shape.
- After bleaching is finished and the wood is dry, sand *with* the grain—by machine, then by hand (120 grit)—to remove cross-grain scratches. Take special care *not* to misshape the "round" of the mast by sanding aggressively or lingering at beauty marks.
- On square spars, sand with the direction of the grain on all grits, using an orbital finishing sander (the Porter-Cable half-sheet sander works best for holding the surface flat and mow-

ing through long stretches quickly). Before moving on to finish sanding (120 grit), run an 80-grit sandpaper–wrapped 2 x 4 block over the flat planes to knock down any high spots and bring the lows flush.

- Complete sanding work with a fine (220-grit) hand-sanding.

sealing/varnishing

- Which varnish? For sealing and buildup coats, use a good, high-solids varnish. When you reach the final three coats, switch to a varnish that is rated for high abrasion, making sure it has a high-grade UV package (see chapter 13 for specific candidates).
- To speed application, varnish in teams: one person (using a *foam* roller) rolls on the varnish, "round the stick" in successive laps, while the other tips off the laps. This helps answer the question "where to leave off?" and prevents "brushing seams" in the dried finish.
- To seal, thin the first coat to 2 parts varnish to 1 part speed-drying solvent. (Use only solvents recommended by the varnish manufacturer.)

- Apply sealer, then allow to dry at least 4 hours (but not overnight). Then, without sanding, apply a second coat thinned 4 to 1, using the same speed-drying solvent. Allow 12 to 24 hours to dry.
- Sand after the second coat, and between all remaining coats, using 220-grit paper.
- After coat 3, reinstall the track and mask it completely. Turn the mast over and set it, track down, on the sawhorses. You'll be "Braille varnishing" at the resting points, but with dedication nothing comes away bare. Halfway through the varnish schedule, move the whole mast forward or back 6 inches, to give at least four full access coats to the spots directly above the sawhorses.
- For buildup coats, apply varnish full strength, one coat per day, thinning only with a companion brushing solvent to ease brushing in the heat—no more than a capful of thinner per cup of varnish.
- After coat 7, allow at least one day between coats for the varnish to cure.
- After coat 10, allow 2 to 3 days for the varnish to cure before

restepping the mast. Ask the rigging crew to be sensitive to the delicate condition of the new finish (and watch them collapse in hysterics . . .)

the spreaders

- When the spreaders have five coats of varnish on them, stop varnishing the tops but continue applying coats to the sides and bottom, through ten coats total.
- After the final varnish coat has cured for at least two days, mask along the top edge of the spreaders, using 3M Safe Release tape (see chapter 13) and *paint* the spreader tops with a high-quality *white* marine enamel. Carefully remove the tape. Allow to dry one full day, then mask again and apply a second coat of paint.

varnishing from a bosun's chair

TWO CRITICAL REMINDERS

1. Don't waste your time or the time of your "support staff" gearing up for this job, only to get to the top of the mast and *discover* (because you ignored the advice about making an inspection trip in *advance* of the perfect varnishing day) that the finish is too far gone to be refreshed from the chair. Know what conditions you will be facing before you gear up for the first prep ride.

2. Unless the finish is in damned excellent shape (common sense will tell you what that is—maybe three or four broken-down spots, maximum) the mast should come down for the work. Otherwise, up you go! TIP: Read this entire section before planning the project.

preparing the crew AND yourself

- Get a *very* good night's sleep, and bring nutritious sustenance to the job, to bank the highest possible reserves of energy.
- Line up the strongest, most *trustworthy* "winch ape" you can find, for the job of pulling you up the mast—someone who brings both brawn and brains to the assignment.
- Eliminate "worrying about being dropped" from the stress of the job. Before you clip the halyard onto your chair, establish "communication rules" with your helper. Most important,

agree to *look at each other* and speak loudly enough to be heard clearly whenever you need to communicate.

- Set up "reply protocols." For example, when I wish to be lowered, here's how the exchange goes:

RJW *(giving the 1-minute warning):* "One minute to lower."
APE: "OK."
RJW *(after 1 minute):* "Down, please."
APE: "OK; *untying* . . . "
RJW *(clutching mast, just to be safe):* "OK."
APE: "Going down."
RJW *(loosening grip on mast):* "OK."
Ape lowers me to desired level, at which point I say:
RJW *(clutching the mast again):* "Stop!"
APE: "OK!" *(and, once he's tied me off)* "Secure!"
RJW: "Thank you!"

what to wear

It can be a warm, sunny day at dock level, and at the same time with the slightest breeze at the top of the mast, you can turn into an icicle. Wear long pants or sweatpants (ones you don't care about slopping up with varnish, because you will . . .) with thick leggings for padding at the knees. Take a jacket and stocking cap, and send them down later if you decide they're superfluous. Never wear black-soled shoes; thick wool socks, pulled *over* your shoes, are best.

the bosun's chair

- Use the roomiest bosun's chair you can get your hands on, preferably one with a rigid seat built in. This keeps your fanny from going to sleep from hours of restricted circulation. If you are thinking of having a chair custom made, I highly recommend calling the Schattauer brothers in Seattle and asking for one just like the one they made for us (see chapter 13 for details).
- If you own a chair fairly simple in design, add a large D-ring on each side, to which you can clip containers for materials and tie extension cords and bungeed accessories.
- Never use a snap shackle to attach the chair to the halyard; use only locking carabiners, the kind used for mountain climbing.

preparing the chair/materials—first trip

loading the chair

- In a lightweight gallon-size bucket, attached with a shock cord to the extra D-ring, stow all but solvent-soaked rags:
    - A lightweight orbital sander (I use my Ryobi), tying the cord onto the D-ring, double-knotted 1 foot beyond arm's length
    - Five clean baby diapers soaked in naphtha (best for quicker drying) or mineral spirits, rolled up individually in a heavy plastic bag
    - A 1-inch Red Devil hook scraper, presharpened
    - Sandpaper—range of grits, cut for sander and for hand-sanding
    - Two foam rubber sanding sponges
    - Five dry baby diapers or clean cotton shop rags, rolled up
    - Nitrile gloves
    - A dust mask
    - Snacks (protein bars, Gatorade, apple quarters, cheese . . .)
    - Sunglasses and visor

- Create a fanny bag—*duct-tape* a doubled paper grocery bag, cuffed 6 inches at the top, to the back of the chair seat, for spent sandpaper and solvent rags
- Tie (at the female end) a 50-foot extension cord onto the same D-ring as the sander

the first trip—prepping the mast

- Before you begin the ascent, assign your Winch Ape the deck-level work (everything from 6 feet up the mast, on down) to be done as you labor aloft. Otherwise, he or she will be sitting around between hoistings, daydreaming and getting fat.
- On your way *up* the first time—wearing nitrile gloves—wipe down the entire mast with solvent-soaked rags. Have yourself pulled up in continuous, brief stops as you do this.
- When you reach the top, start sanding (using the scraper first to fair old drips or broken-down areas).
- Sanding grits: If the varnish is in decent shape, 320 grit provides an adequate tooth. If the last coat had many brush marks, you can use the orbital with 320 grit, but sand lightly (nothing coarser, or you will cut immediately through the finish). If sand-

ing out lap lines by hand, use 220 grit. If fairing broken-down spots after dislodging lifted varnish with a scraper, use 120 grit, then soften the scratch with 320 grit.

- If the finish on the top side of the spreaders is fairly gone (which is often the case), scrape off as much varnish as possible, and then sand with 80 to 120 grit to fair the surface. Wipe down and plan a return trip to them immediately after you finish sanding the rest of the mast.

- When you complete the sanding of each area within your reach, wipe off the dusty residue with a *clean,* thinner-soaked rag, then again with a clean, *dry* diaper. Then give your helper the call to let you down, dropping just far enough to extend your hand up to where you left off sanding above.

- As you work, stow thinner-soaked rags between uses back in their plastic bag, inside the fanny bag—even if they are not spent. Keeping them tucked away nearby exposes you unnecessarily to fumes, and if solvent leaches through your clothes, you can end up with a burn.

- A note on that fanny bag: If you don't fold a deep enough cuff, it is difficult to reach back into the depth of the bag to retrieve things, for fear of flipping over backward. A 6-inch cuff is minimum.

- Don't toss things down to the deckhand. These items will land, more often than not, in the water, and fetching them gets to be a waste of your helper's time. A messenger line with a small bucket attached is a wise thing to set up at the start, for sending things back and forth throughout your time aloft.

- Work your way down the mast doing this sanding-and-wiping-down work. When finished with the whole prep, give the entire boat—all but the mast—a quick hosing down to remove the light layer of dust that cascades from above during sanding.

- If there is enough time in the finishing day (2 hours from the setting dew), and the spreader tops *have* been scraped bare, have your helper do the deck rinsing while you tend to those denuded spreaders. Mix a small pot of varnish with its fast-drying solvent (2:1), and transfer it to a container as described in Preparing the Varnish, below. Go back up to the spreaders with a foam brush and a tack cloth, and apply a seal coat to the bare surfaces. Apply no more than one coat, to ensure drying by the next day.

the second trip—the varnishing ride

loading the chair

- Create another "fanny bag" at the back of the bosun's chair and stow these materials inside until needed:

   Two mineral spirits–soaked rags, rolled up in a heavy plastic bag

   Eight quarter sheets 220-grit sandpaper

   Four each: 1-, 2-, and 3-inch Poly-Brushes in a large Ziploc bag

   Two 1-inch chip brushes

   Two fresh, fully opened and crumpled tack cloths

   One ¾-inch extended-use masking tape (partial roll is best for space)

   Two pairs latex exam gloves

   Nitrile gloves

   Snacks (caviar on toast points, foie gras, champagne . . .)

   Sunglasses and visor

   Varnish in squeeze bottles (see below for preparation)

   A large Ziploc bag, attached at the secondary D-ring

what to wear

Dress in the same getup as for the first ride, but add a sassy little scarf for long hair *and* a painter's cap. Wear a lint-free jacket or down vest under a nylon shell, and large, thick wool socks pulled over your shoes to protect the prepped mast from shoe scrapes.

preparing the varnish . . .

- Using a 2-foot length of ⅛-inch shock cord for each, secure a noose about an inch below the lid on two old-fashioned new ketchup squeeze containers, then wrap two or three times over the noose with ½-inch electrical tape to prevent the cord from slipping off the bottles.

- Thin varnish for brushing, straining into a clean paper bucket and adding no more than a capful per cup of brushing solvent. Bend the edge of the bucket to form a pouring spout, and transfer the varnish into the prepared ketchup bottles. Secure the lids tightly to prevent leaking, but don't overtighten or the lids will pop off.

- When you get situated in the bosun's chair, tie the shock cord of one bottle onto the D-ring attached to the halyard and stow the bottle in a side pocket on the bosun's chair. Stow the spare bottle inside the fanny bag until needed. (This, in addition to the rigid seat, is what makes our Schattauer chair so wonderful. They designed a side pocket in the shape of a pop can, which holds a varnishing squirt bottle perfectly upright and uncrushed.)

preparing the boat and environs

- Spread drop cloths over the entire boat, boom, and mainsail.
- Either make provisions to cover neighboring boats, or warn skippers of your plans to varnish from above and the inevitability of flying drops. If you haven't sufficient drop cloths to protect the neighbors' boats, instruct your helper to be at the ready with mineral spirits when trouble hits. Inspect neighboring boats at the end of the project for any drops that went undetected during the project.

going up

- Wear nitrile gloves as you go up, and quickly and lightly wipe the mast with solvent-moistened rags. Don't stop as you go; just have your helper winch you up slowly as you wipe.
- When you reach the spreaders, stop and lightly sand the sealed tops; wipe down lightly. Varnish the spreaders from the outer tips inward, first on the tops, and then on the bottoms.
- *Do not save varnishing the spreaders for the trip down.* It will interrupt the continuity of the varnishing on the mast.
- Remember as you ascend, and again as you *descend*, not to step on the wet spreaders.

coming down

- When you reach the top of the mast, mask off any fittings likely to get slopped with varnish, using ¾-inch tape.
- Tack, down to waist level, and begin varnishing from the top down, using the chip brushes for tight areas beneath the masthead. If possible without messing things up, pull the tape as you complete this area, and stuff it into the Ziploc bag attached to the D-ring at your side.
- If you know you will be returning to the top on a third day, perhaps to finish work on the spreader tops, leave the masking tape in place until then. Just make sure, if you do so, that it is an extended-use tape and not normal painter's grade.
- Keep a stocking-covered shoe between your lifting halyard

and the mast at all times. *Do not remove that foot* until you arrive at the bottom of the mast. This prevents the halyard from slapping against wet varnish.

- Figure on spending about twenty minutes—at least—on the first couple of feet of varnishing. This is tedious work at the very top, and requires time and patience to work around all the impediments and attachments.

- Once you get out from under the constrictive web of rigging at the top of the mast, the varnishing will seem to fly by comparison. Work your way down methodically, brushing each stroke in an upward motion back into the wet edge that preceded it.

the third (and possibly fourth) trip

- If you are planning *two* refresher coats, allow the first coat to dry for 5 days, then go at it again, repeating the drills for rides 1 and 2, skipping the initial thinner wipe-down, and prepping lightly with 320 grit.

- Don't be tempted to *begin* varnishing past midday, or the dew will "fog" the varnish that goes on by the time you've reached the deck.

- If you are going back up *only* to finish the spreaders, you can go up after 48 hours, but commune gingerly with the newly varnished mast as you head up for the spreader work.

finishing the spreaders
loading the chair

- Create another fanny bag at the back of the bosun's chair and stow these materials therein:
    Four quarter sheets 320-grit sandpaper
    A mineral spirits–moistened rag in a heavy plastic bag
    White high-gloss marine enamel—full strength (in a squeeze bottle, prepared as above for varnish)
    A roll of ¾-inch masking tape
    A clean tack cloth
    Three 2-inch Poly-Brushes
    Two sticks Wrigley's Spearmint gum
    A pair of latex exam gloves
    Sunglasses and visor
    A large Ziploc bag, attached to the secondary D-ring

- Take the express elevator directly to the top, to pull any tape left behind after varnishing.
- Drop down to the spreaders, and mask along the top edges. Lightly sand the tops; wipe down, tack, and then paint the tops with a generous but not overly thick coat of paint. Remove the tape as you complete each side, and stuff it into the Ziploc attached at your side.

two explanations and a word to the wise . . .

Why white paint on spreaders? Varnish, at spreader level—with no regular access for maintenance—will only immediately peel off. The white paint reflects the sun's rays and provides long-term protection for the wood. Never skip the first varnish coats, though, because the wood needs a decent seal to keep the paint adhered to the surface.

Why ketchup bottles? I hate the panic that overtakes me when I take an open container of *anything*—varnish, paint, Dom Perignon —aloft. The incidence of "dropsy" increases in direct proportion to the height at which we work. A foam brush is one thing (and why do you think I call for so *many* of those?). Dropping an open quart of Clipper Clear from 70 feet up would render my entire psyche a sticky mess. A squeeze bottle metes out a perfect measure of varnish onto the foam brush. And, given its attachment to me by its shock cord (available by the foot in most marine chandleries), *dropping the varnish* means only nonchalantly leaning over, retrieving the tethered bottle, and continuing on—boat and nerves relatively unscathed.

Sometimes the chair should remain in the dock box: If there's even a moderate wind, the job will be twice as hard to do, take three times as long, and end up four times as ugly when finished. You will also be frozen to the bone by the time you reach the deck, and the winch ape will have to peel you out of the bosun's chair. Wait for an ideal weekend forecast. Better yet, play hooky on the first set of beautiful *weekdays* that comes along. Because the weekend, regardless of climate, is when everyone is heading out to sail or coming back into port. All those wakes can make you feel like an ant at the top of a metronome. Dizzier than a Gillespie, I promise you'll be!

part **3** tools, materials, and resources

chapter **12**

you can

never be too rich or

have too many tools . . .

On our second date, David walked into what he expected would be my garage, and discovered

a 400-square-foot room full of tools.
Hand tools. Power tools.
A dust collector.

He gasped.
We were married eleven months later.

I confess it: I'm a tool junkie.
Here's my **Brightwork** tool collection. Other brands work for other people; these are my favorites.

This brightwork artist's *"quintessential tool collection"*

#1 the sanders bag: Porter-Cable Speed-Bloc sander with extra "keys," Porter Cable random orbit sander, Ryobi one-sixth-sheet sander, 25-foot extension cord, Fein detail sander

#2 the heat stripping bag: Easy Gun heat gun, hook scrapers (Murphy, Red Devil), stainless steel dental picks, fine Red Devil mill file, X-Acto knife set with extra blades

#3 the boat prep bag: Bosch cordless drill with assortment of driver bits, box of 1-quart Ziploc bags, Sharpie laundry pen, assortment of 3M masking tapes (in Ziploc bags), razor blade

scraper, boxes of single-edged razor blades, bungee cord assortment, *Instant Weather Forecasting* by Alan Watts

#4 the sanding accoutrements bag: Hard rubber sanding blocks, sponge sanding blocks, 2x4 wood sanding blocks, cork sanding blocks, sandpaper cutter, counter brush

#5 the varnishing toys bag: All sealed, individually, in Ziploc bags: Hardman Double/Bubble epoxy packets with stir sticks, pint paper buckets, cone varnish strainers, tack cloths, Poly-Brushes (range of sizes), retired cotton diapers, industrial shop rags, collapsible ice pick, paint-can opener, rubber mallet, metal slotted stirring wands, Wrigley's Extra/Polar Ice gum—PlenTPak (tastes *almost* like Beeman's!)

#6 the bleaching bag: Nitrile gloves, eye shields, plastic funnel, utility knife with extra blades, duct tape, construction rain suit, deck boots

#7 the personal comfort bag: Knee pads, nitrile gloves, 3M dust-mist masks (in Ziploc bag), 2 dozen latex exam gloves, foam ear protectors, eye shields, first-aid kit

#8 the hand tools bag: Wood chisels, screwdrivers, adjustable wrench, pliers, awl, shop scissors, Tim Allen finishing hammer, 25-foot Stanley Leverlock tape, drill bit assortment

and in their own little universe . . .

- Craftsman wet-dry vacuum with brush nozzle, crevice tool, and standard floor-sweeping attachments
- Porter-Cable half-sheet heavy-duty finishing sander
- Plastic Multi-File box of sandpaper—range of grits (see chapter 13)

If you are deeply involved in brightwork and/or woodworking pursuits and have as many tools as I do, no doubt you have a system of order already in place. If you are just beginning to amass a collection, I urge you to organize your tools (and materials) in this fashion, in separate heavy-duty canvas bags, according to specific roles they play in your work. That way, they can be identified at a glance, and you can grab the one you need for the job you're heading off to do, without rummaging through the whole shebang for a tool to handle the specific task at hand.

As you become settled into the logic of those bags, you will also realize more readily what is missing from any particular one.

Keep a checklist inside each bag so you can track what belongs where, and what needs replacing.

. . . of course, anybody can amass the quintessential tool collection. *it takes a true aficionado to live by "the rules"*

I confess to the occasional inclination toward mania when someone abuses my tools.
If you'd like to be a tool lover's pal, I highly encourage adopting The Tools Rules.
There are only a few . . .

the tools rules

1. Don't loan tools.
2. Don't borrow tools.
3. Organize your tool bag.
4. Use the right tool for the job.
5. Never leave your tools in the rain.
6. Always clean a tool when you mess it up.
7. If you break a tool, fix/replace it within a week.
8. Don't ever leave your tools where they can be stolen.
9. When you're finished with a tool, put it back where it belongs.
10. Buy the best-quality tool, regardless of how much more it costs
    (especially if it's a gift . . .).

P.S. When directed toward your spouse, it's nice to preface rules with "please."

the sandpaper cutter: *how to make (and use) one*

To get perfect quarters for your Speed-Bloc, or perfect halves for your big finishing sander, or sixths for your old Ryobi, or just to cut up multiple sheets of paper lickety-split, add this home-made tool to your collection.

1. Cut a piece of particleboard, or plywood that won't warp, to measure 8 by 14 inches.

2. Attach a medium-toothed hacksaw blade to the board—teeth facing right—1 inch from the right-hand long edge of the board.

   - Use stainless steel #6 ³⁄₈-inch pan-head sheet-metal screws.
   - Drive the screws through a #10 flat washer, placed under the blade at the hole at each end.

3. With an indelible marker (medium-point Sharpie laundry markers are best), draw three lines parallel to, and to the left of, the blade, at these distances from the *toothed* edge: 3 inches, 4½ inches, 5½ inches.

When using the cutter, put pressure on the blade with two fingers while you tear the paper upward with your other hand.

   Always tear paper *grit side down*, to prolong the life of the blade. **TIP:** Save a ton of refinishing time by learning to cut multiple sheets at once.

about sanders: *the brightwork grind!*

orbital finishing sanders

I own two sizes of orbital sander, both made by Porter-Cable. The quarter-sheet Speed-Bloc is heavy and built like a little tank. This model has been around for decades and is still the finest sander on the market, in my opinion. Do not confuse it with that company's orbital model called the PalmGrip sander, or any other quarter-sheet finishing sander, for that matter. Most other sanders are half the price of the Speed-Bloc and less than half the tool. If you own only one sander, make it a Porter-Cable Speed-Bloc. **TIP:** Load stacks of precisely cut sandpaper quarters, and then peel off the sheets as the sandpaper wears out. *Plus, tie the key to the cord!* The Porter-Cable half-sheet finishing sander is exactly what its name suggests and is another sander to own if you anticipate doing much deck sanding or expansive work, or if you plan to go into the brightwork business. If you're doing just

your own boat and you don't want to commit the money for this sander, at least find out where to rent one if you need to mow down a deck. It cuts sanding time in half on a vast acreage of teak. **TIP:** Load sandpaper *tightly!* The one biggest thing to impart about orbital sanders in general is the importance of allowing the motor to rev fully up to speed before setting the sander down against the work—and, once there, not bearing down hard on the sander. This reduces sanding scars and extends the life of the tool.

random orbit sanders

The random orbit sander is a brilliant stroke of the engineering pen. Combining the orbit of finishing sanders with the spin of disc sanders gives us a completely new sander that cuts through wood and oily finishes quickly and with a minimum of orbital scarring. The only downsides for brightwork application are 1) by design, the disc shape precludes working up into the corners of trims and perpendicular joinery, and 2) the cost of the hook/loop and stick-on abrasives is considerably higher than that of sandpaper sheets used on traditional clamp-loaded orbitals. For these reasons, I still gravitate toward a Speed-Bloc for much of the detail—and certainly all of the "between coats"—work in refinishing. For people in the business who factor the cost of

materials against the cost of labor, a random orbit sander is a "must-own" in the tools inventory. For the do-it-yourself brightwork artist, this sander is a luxury to own, one that should not supplant the Speed-Bloc if the tool budget is limited. I have two random orbits: one palm size, with a built-in dust collector, and one larger, early-generation model, with a dust-collection attachment. They are both made by Porter-Cable. *Many* tool manufacturers make random orbit sanders. The good ones are the ones that are not cheap. **TIP:** Contrary to standard orbital sander rules, always rest the sanding head *on* the work before turning on the sander.

detail sanders (aka profile sanders . . .): The Fein Company was the trailblazer in what has to be the ultimate luxury in sanders. This triangular-head sander oscillates into the most inaccessible reaches of finish work, saving untold hours of hand-sanding and keeping things like louvered doors from looking like good candidates for firewood. **TIP:** If you buy one, treat yourself to a Fein MultiMaster. The kit includes the tool body with sanding head and sandpaper, plus a scraper head and a flush-cut saw blade. If you have deck seam work to do, Fein also makes a reefing blade attachment for this tool that removes seam caulking cleanly and in record time. (Go to feinus.com on the Internet for more information on the tool itself. To purchase, if you can't find it locally, go to coastaltools.com.)

and finally, *the tools obituaries . . .*

It is with genuine sadness that I report that production of two of my favorite tools has ceased. One is a victim of the corporate bottom line. The other fades from the landscape with the passing of its inventor.

The Ryobi sixth-sheet palm sander, the only orbital machine made with a hard rubber pad, is no longer being made. It was petite yet efficient, and the perfect way to wet-sand oil into large stretches of wood without losing an arm from exhaustion. (If you try to wet-sand with any other orbital, the pad will disintegrate before you go through the first sheet of sandpaper.) The Ryobi's smaller size also made it the perfect auxiliary tool for flat-sanding in tiny places.

I own two of these; maybe I'll put the older one on eBay. Starting bid: $47,000.

The Easy Gun heat gun is also no longer available. This was one of those rare tools shepherded into the retail world by the man who designed it, and it ultimately put to shame anything that had the audacity to sit next to it on the shelf. After Reese Kennedy died, his sweet wife and daughters continued production for as long as it made sense to do so. But the Easy Gun finally became too expensive to produce, the girls moved on to lives of their own, and now Joanne has grandbabies to spoil. So, those of us lucky enough to own that spectacular little red gun, compact and lightweight enough to be mistaken for a hair dryer, yet capable of reducing varnish to a quick bubbling ash (1,200°F!), must guard our riches and resist the inclination to loan it out. I don't really have a substitute to recommend; my best advice is to

search for a used Easy Gun, or some other model that will heat up to at least 1,100°F, with an element that promises to last beyond one project. Either way means an investment somewhere around a hundred dollars. (Don't waste your money on a cheapie. An inexpensive heat gun is like a McDonald's hamburger wrapper. You know the minute you take delivery that you'll be throwing it away.)

I own two Easy Guns as well; maybe I'll put the older one on eBay. Starting bid: $97,000.

Tools are like the people we love:

Treasure them—you never know when you won't be able to get your hands on them again.

13

it's a
materials world . . .

Madonna was totally referring to her brightwork refinishing materials in that song *right? like, for her yacht?*

The brightwork artist's "materials world" is one that threatens constant revolution. It's a ceaseless tide of product development that can be as brilliant and inspired as a set of Paul Simon lyrics, or as shameless and transparent as Madonna's stage attire. "Change" is both muse and anthem in the aisles of the marine supply trades. There is only one constant in that world, a phenomenon that resides in the brightwork materials aisle that goes back to the days of the Pharaohs: someone will always be claiming to have come up with the product that Ends All Need To Varnish . . .

The materials named throughout this book are, with few exceptions, ones that I have long used. If I have *not* mentioned the name of something that a particular reader passionately embraces, that omission means nothing more than that it is not a product I happen to use. Period. (I can't use them *all*, can I?) As always, I beg my students, readers, and fellow brightwork artisans to remember that the best products are nothing more than the ones with which each person has had success. In the way that it is foolhardy to argue with loved ones over politics, it is an exercise in silliness to argue over someone's choice in varnish or deck treatment or chosen brand of bleach. If it works for them, don't try to fix it.

And so, without apology or invitation to argument, here are the materials for which I am still crazy after all these years . . .

but first, a word about suppliers . . .

Some people live in places where there exists neither a local chandlery nor a marine supply chain. For these folks, the Internet is a godsend. It's a rare company that does not have a presence on the World Wide Web. Wherever possible, I have included web addresses along with traditional resource information to make finding materials easier for people in remote ports.

an Internet gem!

One spectacular website is that of Fisheries Supply. It has the most extensive inventory of brightwork materials, laid out in the most logical way, of any marine supply resource I've found on the Internet. For nearly every product named in this book, go to **www.fisheriessupply.com** and shop by "department" (*after*, of course, you've checked with your local chandlery . . .).

the various products of the brightwork trade, sorted by function . . .

bleaching . . .

TE-KA A&B WOOD CLEANER

Te-Ka A&B is a two-step bleaching system. The A, which does the nasty bleaching work, is a sodium hydroxide solution; the B, which stops the bleaching action of the A and brightens the "cooked" wood back to normal color, is a phosphoric acid solution. Te-Ka eats right through paint, can score the wax job on gelcoat, and burns unprotected skin. Pull up the full material safety data sheets (MSDS) on the company's website, and use this product with great respect for safety warnings. It's a chemical bully, but when the job calls for powerful measures, it's the quickest route to clean wood.

Travaco Products division of ITW Philadelphia Resins
130 Commerce Drive
Montgomeryville, Pennsylvania
    18936
215 855 8450
Fax 215 855 4688
E-mail sales@itwprc.com
www.marinetex.com/

TEAK WONDER

Teak Wonder is not actually bleach but a heavy detergent with an added enzyme. The enzyme is the essential ingredient in this product, and the key to success in using it is keeping the cleaner in a lather as it sits on the wood, which heightens the efficiency of the enzyme by shielding it from sunlight. Teak Wonder comes packaged with a brightener—a citric acid solution designed to stop the action of the residual detergent. Do not skip using this part, despite suggestion in the instructions that it is optional.

Teak Wonder
T-Jett Marine
14260 S.W. 136th Street, #10
Miami, Florida 33186
305 252 1210
Fax 305 252 1210

DALY'S A&B BLEACH

This is a wonderful product for bleaching woods that cannot be treated to a wholesale rinse—on fixed cabin soles, for example. The two parts are mixed together according to the strength of bleaching solution desired. The A is a sodium silicate; the B is hydrogen peroxide.

Daly's
3525 Stone Way North
Seattle, Washington 98103
800 735 7019; 206 633 4200
Fax 206 632 2565
E-mail info@dalyspaint.com
www.dalyspaint.com/

OXALIC ACID

An inexpensive means of removing mildew or water stains from bare, untreated wood. For spot-bleaching, make a paste; neutralize with borax, vinegar, or soda ash. For a large area, mix 16 ounces oxalic acid in 1 gallon hot water. Neutralize with 3 ounces borax in 1 gallon hot water.

TSP—TRISODIUM PHOSPHATE

A bleaching salt; adding this to the Lemon Joy in your swabbing bucket is a good way to keep mildew from settling into your teak decks.

Both of these generic bleaching products are available at most hardware, home improvement, and drugstores.

stripping . . .

CITRISTRIP PAINT AND VARNISH STRIPPING GEL

This stripper contains a citrus distillate known as d-limonene, which gives it a delicious orange scent, the same stuff you find in citrus hand cleaners that remove tar and paint. But what also makes this work as an effective stripper is a biodegradable, non-flammable solvent called n-methyl-2-pyrrolidone. This stripper, with a slight measure of patience, single-handedly replaces the need for exposure to methyene chloride chemical strippers. It's also *widely* available, at home improvement centers across the land, and far less expensive than most marine strippers.

Citristrip
Wm Barr Consumer Products Group
2105 Channel Avenue
Memphis, Tennessee 38113
800 235 3546
E-mail citristrip@wmbarr.com
www.citristrip.com (a great
    little site, with a "product
    knowledge" instruction
    video and a user's forum)

sanding . . .

SANDPAPER

3M is the King of the Sandpaper World. Don't waste your money on paper made by anyone else. When you choose from 3M's vast selection of papers, you make your selection on the basis of two features: grit and paper weight. Dry sandpapers come in three weights from light to heavy: A, C, and D, and—for marine use especially—P. Wet-or-dry papers come in two weights: A and C. Grits used in brightwork projects can range from 50 to 600; it's wise to have a full range on hand at all times throughout a major refinishing schedule.

Above all, every reference to the use of sandpaper in this book, and inferences to grits of paper (with the exception of wet-or-dry paper in oiling) presupposes the use of only the 3M Fre-Cut line of papers. This kind of sandpaper has a zinc stearate coating, which helps prevent clogging when used on oily woods and finishes. You will know whether you have this paper by looking on the back of every sheet. It will say Fre-Cut, and the gritty side will either be a silver-white or a gold color, depending on which variation the chandlery has chosen to carry. The gold is Resinite Fre-Cut, so named because the grit is affixed with resin rather than glue, on special P weight paper developed specifically for marine environments, and as such is less inclined to curl in humid air. One significant difference between Tri-M-Ite Fre-Cut silver and Resinite Fre-Cut gold sandpapers: the latter is almost one full grit range sharper than its silver same-grit counterpart. Factor this in when shifting between the two papers.

The most economical way to buy sandpaper is by the sleeve, in 9-by-11-inch sheets. On finishing grits (120 on up), a sleeve is typically 100 sheets. On shaping grits (60 to 100), a 50-sheet sleeve is the normal package. The neatest, most efficient way to keep a full inventory of grits is to place them—still in their original sleeve—filed in grit order in a hard plastic Multi-File. You al-ways know when you're low on any grit, and the sheets stay flat and dry until the day you pull them out to work.

3M also makes all their Fre-Cut papers in Stik-It and Hook 'n Loop configurations, for use on some orbital, random orbit, and detail sanders. These papers become considerably more expensive in these configurations, but when these tools are called for, it's time to get out your wallet and be thankful that the product has been adapted across the technological board.

3M
800 771 7049
www.mmm.com

intermediate prep . . .

HARDMAN DOUBLE/BUBBLE EPOXY

This is one of those brilliant bits of packaging that makes an otherwise inconvenient material an indispensable part of the brightwork materials kit bag. The Hardman epoxy "double bubble" is a little two-chambered aluminum packet with the perfect measure of resin and catalyst, meant to be torn open and mixed together with a popsicle stick (provided) to create about a tablespoon of material. It's the perfect portion to mix with ½ teaspoon wood flour for little topping-up projects at joints prior to varnishing. If your local chandlery doesn't carry it, tell them you want it. They'll thank you for the introduction.

> Elementis Specialties
> Ordering: 888 442 7362, ext. 3773; 973 751 3000
> Customer Service: 800 418 5197
> www.elementis-specialties.com

CLEAR PENETRATING EPOXY SEALERS

I don't personally employ clear penetrating epoxy sealers (CPES) (for example, Smith & Company) or any other product with an epoxy undercoat in my finishing regimen. Aside from simply being a purist in my varnishing, I am opposed in principle, and in practice, to exposing myself when it's not absolutely nonnegotiable to materials that are inherently toxic to use. These sorts of products, typically about 30 percent solids and 70 percent solvent, are full of isocyanates and low-flash-point solvents, and are as toxic as anything you could encounter in the finishing world. Prudent users need to heed the safety warnings about exposure to the solvents in penetrating epoxies, and take measures to protect themselves, ideally by using air-supplied respirators and/or setting up foolproof systems of air movement—even when working outdoors. The line from the California Product Liability code says it all: "This product is inherently unsafe. It cannot be made safe."

That said, there are many people who do use these products and who believe strongly in their efficacy. In the interest of balance, I encourage all finishers to become familiar with this concept and decide for themselves whether epoxy sealers have a place in their own brightwork program. Just take with a grain of salt the disingenuous "modern replacement for varnish" or "makes varnishing obsolete" claims that typically adorn the labels on such products. The fact is, epoxy sealers *are* still meant to be varnished over or are themselves, by definition, "varnish products" (albeit varnishes made with resins and solvents that are different from those in traditional varnishes). In the final analysis, they *will* have to be maintained, and the brightwork *will* eventually one day have to be refinished again . . .

For an FYI resource on penetrating epoxy as a *concept*, go to the following address on the Internet:

www.epoxyproducts.com/penetrating4u.html

For information about the original CPES, you will find a lengthy infomercial at Smith and Company's website.

Smith and Company
5100 Channel Avenue
Richmond, California 94804
800 234 0330
E-mail smi3th@smithandcompany.org
www.smithandcompany.org

oiling . . .

Before any mention of oil products, two salient *oiling tips* are in order:

1. Never oil with a bristle brush; always use a *foam* brush.
2. Never oil with a rag—you get a half coat at best.

There are a bazillion oil formulas on the market. Some are good; some are garbage.

DALY'S SEAFIN TEAK OIL is the only one I ever bother with, because it is made from the highest-quality tung oil and is wonderfully compatible with almost any varnish you could imagine applying over it, if you are using oil as a sealer. I wet-sand in SeaFin as a sealer before varnishing on teak. It is also the best-quality penetrating tung oil formula for wet-sanding oil in interior finishing. I do not recommend SeaFin—or any *other* oil formula—for exterior finishing.

See the Daly's listing on page 149 for company information.

BOILED LINSEED OIL

When raw linseed oil is heated to 500°F, its drying properties are enhanced. The oil dries in 12 to 15 hours, as opposed to 4 to 6 *days* in its raw state. Unfortunately, the cooking darkens the oil dramatically, so current purveyors of linseed oil have taken to inducing faster drying times by adding metallic oxides to a small portion of heated oil, which is then added to a greater portion of oil, which remains uncooked. This is the product I use when mixing the sealer described in chapter 7 for the boiled linseed oil soak. Boiled linseed oil is carried in many woodworking stores and chandleries, under myriad labels. They're all pretty much the same, so I encourage buying whichever is handiest.

RAGS RAGS RAGS!

When doing any kind of oiling work, the best rags are ones that are lint-free. My absolute favorites have been the used blue cotton surgical towels my dad gave us after someone at the local hospital passed them (laundered, of course) along to him. No longer sterile for medical use, they're perfect for buffing off wet-sanded oil and wiping down oil-soaked wood. My other favorite oiling "rags" are retired diapers and the bulk cotton shop rags often sold at big supply chains like Costco and Home Depot.

ELEPHANT BRAND FINE OR EXTRAFINE BRONZE WOOL

This is the ideal way to rub oil into wood to maintain an oil finish. Never mistakenly substitute *steel* wool; the slivers will leave rust marks everywhere. To extend the life of a bronze wool pad once used, store it in a lidded mason jar or, for short periods of time, in a Ziploc bag.

taping . . .

In addition to being King of the Sandpaper World, 3M is also Emperor of the Masking Tapes Empire. Regardless of the savings, never be tempted to use a lesser brand of masking tape. You'll regret the error the second you try to peel the cheap stuff off.

These are the four tapes made by 3M that are standard for use in brightwork projects.

#2040 PAINTER'S MASKING TAPE: This is their general-use crepe paper tape, applicable in everything from sanding work to short-term varnish masking. Never leave this tape on overnight. Work with 1-inch widths, and lay a double thickness when taping off for machine-sanding.

#2070 SAFE RELEASE TAPE: This is a low-tack flat-back tape, best to use when masking over a vulnerable surface like paint; not meant to be left on overnight or used through multiple coats.

#2090 BLUE LONG MASK: This is the industry standard for long-term taping—a crepe paper tape that should come off every third coat to ensure clean removal and a neat varnish edge.

#256 SCOTCHMARK GREEN: Another flat-back tape, meant for medium-term masking. Fine to pull off after two or three coats, but should come off within no more than 7 days.

A fifth tape, **#226 SOLVENT RESISTANT TAPE**, is a coated crepe paper tape that is impervious to solvents—good for that rare occasion when you're stripping chemically next to vulnerable painted surfaces. Test a small piece to make sure it doesn't pull up the paint it's adhered to; if it does, underlay first with #2070, making sure you create a strong edge bond.

four tape tips

- Keep every roll of tape you ever buy in a Ziploc bag, before and after use. This maintains clean, sealable edges for varnishing.
- When taping, hold a razor blade at the spot you mean to tear, and pull the tape up against the blade to leave a clean end.
- Lay tape no closer than $1/16$ inch from a brightwork edge to create a proper varnish seal.
- After using a cheap tape, or leaving #2040 on too long, you can remove the gummy residue with 3M General Purpose Adhesive Remover.

varnishing . . .

TACK CLOTHS

A tack cloth is not the means by which you clean heavy sanding grit and grime from a surface before varnishing. It is your quality-control companion while you varnish an already clean boat. The cleaner the boat is before you begin varnishing, the longer your tack cloth will serve you.

two tack cloth tips

- When tacking, don't *scrub* with the cloth, but rather wipe gently over the varnishing plane, just enough to pick up any particulate matter that has settled since the initial vacuuming and wipe-down.
- Keep a tack cloth in a Ziploc bag between uses to extend the usable life of the cloth.

Gerson Tack Cloth/High Tack Tan—This is the very best tack cloth: supertacky with maximum pickup and holding power.

Louis M. Gerson Company Inc.
15 Sproat Street
Middleboro, Massachusetts 02346
800 225 8623; 508 947 4000
E-mail custserv@gersonco.com
www.gersonco.com

FOAM BRUSHES AND FOAM ROLLERS

Jen Brush Mfg. brushes and rollers are the originals and the *only* ones to use. The Jen Poly-Brush has a wooden handle and a firm plastic square glued inside the foam head to help maintain rigidity. There are many copycats, but no other company uses the caliber of foam in this brush, or delivers the varnish or paint as well as these. Jen Mfg. is the McDonald's of foam brush makers: billions sold! Available just about anywhere you can buy finishing products. To save money, buy them by the box; keep them in a clean, dry place until you need them.

FOAM BRUSH TIP: Dip the brush into the finish no farther than just past the bevel; the brush will load sufficiently over repeated dippings.

VARNISH

I'm a "mate for life" kind of girl (something my former husbands didn't seem to appreciate). I've tried out every varnish that's ever been sold—and a few that have never made it past their company's R&D departments—but I'm inclined to stick with the ones that I *love.* I encourage you to do the same: stick with the ones that *you love.* If you are new to the world of brightwork, take time to get to know a varnish well; be patient with its idiosyncrasies and your own learning curve. Ask people what they know from their own experience with that product. And don't expect things of a varnish that are not possible. Your relationship with your varnish, just like your relationship with your spouse, will be beautiful and satisfying only as long as *you* are prepared to do the hard work.

Before any discussion of "what's the best varnish," it is imperative to promote an understanding of "how to treat *any* varnish."

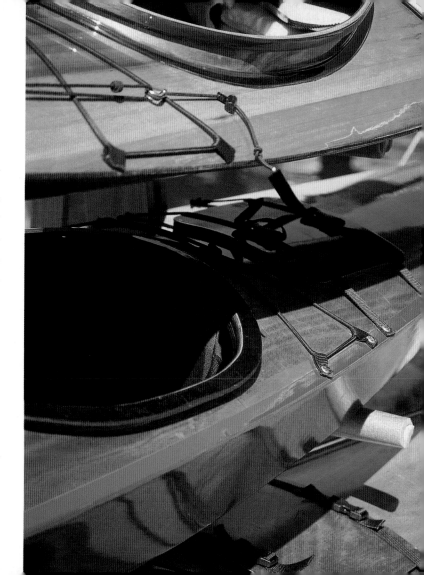

varnish handling tips

- Unless the product specifically states otherwise, never apply more than one coat of varnish per day.
- Varnish is not a James Bond martini: don't shake it, even to redistribute flatteners in satin finishes. Stirring *only!*
- Always pour varnish *and solvents,* even new from the can, through a fresh cone strainer, and rock the mixture gently to combine.
- Never varnish directly from the can; transfer what you are able to use *within an hour* to a clean paper bucket.
- Use an awl or ice pick to poke three holes in the "rim trough" of a newly opened varnish can, to reduce buildup in the rim between pourings.
- Keep a rubber mallet in your varnishing tool bag at all times, and never close a varnish or paint can with any other instrument.
- Don't play junior chemist with your varnish; follow the manufacturer's instructions *faithfully* when adding solvents.
- Store varnish in a place that does not undergo dramatic fluctuations of temperature; store it tightly lidded and *upside down* between uses.

As for "the best varnishes," I'm happy to offer the names of several of great repute, along with the few I call "my favorites." Depending on your level of expertise, your climate, your patience quotient, your wood's disposition, your astrological sign, and your belief in the power of sheer accidental good luck, you may enjoy varying brushes with success in using any of the following (among others):

Epifanes
Woolsey/Z-Spar Captain's and Flagship
Rivale Classic
McCloskey's Bote-Kote
Man O' War

But my *favorites* are

INTERLUX VARNISHES
- #96 Schooner is the crown jewel of the Interlux varnish line, and my all-time favorite spar varnish.
- #60, formerly known only by its generic name Rubbed Effect, is now sold as Goldspar Satin. It's a perfect interior varnish.

- #95 Clipper Clear has a polyurethane resin that makes it ideal for use on masts and other surfaces that are vulnerable to abrasion.

And these varnishes are best combined with their companion Interlux thinners:

- #216 Special Thinner (for accelerating drying)
- #333 Brushing Liquid (for slowing down skinning during application)

> Interlux/International Paint Inc.
> 2270 Morris Avenue
> Union, New Jersey 07083
> 800 468 7589 technical support line
> www.yachtpaint.com/usa (a good website, with access to MSDS and detailed descriptions of each product's particular character)

finally, a few words about the water-based varnish frenzy . . .

It seemed for a while that every varnish maker was rushing to the shelves some water-based varnish formula that (you guessed it) Made Varnishing A Thing Of The Past, and gave the brightwork artist the promise of a full varnish job at the snap of a finger, all within the blink of an eye . . . at no cost to the ozone layer and, oh by the way, they'd also accidentally discovered the cure for cancer and warts and ADD (attention deficit disorder). In other words, lots of pretty new cans of sucker syrup, and a year later a lot of people writing to me asking how to get the ugly stuff off. . . . Bottom line: I've tested and tossed out too much water-based varnish to want a seat on that bandwagon. Until good old-fashioned oleoresinous varnish is outlawed outright, I'm sticking with the real McCoy. (The answer: The water-based stuff that hasn't *flaked* off responds nicely to a heat gun.)

miscellaneous solvents . . .

turpentine: This classic "paint thinner," around since the early days of paint and varnish production, is made by distilling the rosin or "gum" of the longleaf pine tree (hence the name "gum turpentine"). With the advent of coatings made with synthetic resins, this has become a more or less obsolete brushing additive, replaced in wide practice by mineral spirits.

mineral spirits: *Also* known generically as "paint thinner," this is a hydrocarbon distillate with a high flash point, meaning a slow rate of evaporation, which therefore makes it an ideal additive for easing the flow of paint and varnish. The highest-quality mineral spirits are produced by steam distillation, which removes the impurities from the raw solvent. Most varnish makers package a

proprietary form of steam-distilled mineral spirits as a companion "brushing thinner."

lacquer thinner: This is a blend of hot solvents (low flash point) that differs slightly from one company's can to the next. The most important thing for a brightwork artist to know about lacquer thinner is that it has *no* place in a pot of varnish or paint and, aside from being the way to wash methylene chloride stripper dregs from bare wood, it has no place in any course of their work.

acetone: This is a colorless, volatile member of the ketone family of solvents, with a very low flash point. As a utility solvent, it evaporates quickly and is handy for washing surfaces of grease, pencil markings, and other contaminants that might later wreak havoc under a finish.

shellac thinner: This is the industry name for denatured alcohol. It can hasten the drying of bare woods that need to be rinsed with water, by mixing it in equal parts with the rinse water.

Japan drier: Modern formulations sold as "Japan drier" are combinations of any number of metallic driers (cobalt, manganese, etc.) with oils and solvents (typically mineral spirits). This is a solvent that many people toss into their varnish when they want to kick it into drying mode quickly under difficult conditions. I advise sticking with the varnish maker's recommended in-house "catalyzing" thinner—the one typically called out for spray application—in lieu of a generic Japan drier.

3M General Purpose Adhesive Remover: This is a very-high-flash-point solvent packaged by 3M, a cocktail of naphtha, xylene, and benzene, and is an important can to keep on hand for occasional lapses in the timely removal of masking tape. It is also good for removing wax, crayon, silicone, tar, and some oils from gelcoat and wood surfaces. Use it gingerly on Plexiglas or Lexan surfaces.

miscellaneous maintenance materials . . .

chamois: Real chamois skins are the best way to clean brightwork, especially when you're out cruising. Keep a couple good skins on board, and use them first thing in the day to wipe up the dew; this gives you a natural source of fresh water for removing saltwater crystals, which damage the finish.

Always use a chamois wet—never dry. Keep it clean by washing in gentle detergent and rinsing thoroughly, then stretch it into shape for drying.

Murphy Oil Soap and Shaklee's Industrial I: These are both great soaps for washing a boat and cleaning teak decks and brightwork. The Shaklee's is biodegradable yet removes stains on gelcoat and is easy on the brightwork and bare decks. Murphy's is a gentle cleaner for varnish.

Lemon Joy: This common dish soap is ideal for washing decks with salt water while cruising; it is the only soap I know of that will lather in salt water.

Liberty Polish: This metal cleaner and polish was developed in 1920 and is the absolute best formula on the market for restoring the shine to brass, bronze, and stainless steel surfaces on a boat. It's nonflammable, not harmful or caustic to skin, and doesn't leave a residue. Use with a soft, dry cloth—baby diapers are best. Terry cloth can scratch some metals, especially soft brass.

> Liberty Polish
> Delta Industries
> 191 S. Gulph Road
> King of Prussia, Pennsylvania 19406
> 800 435 7338

retired baby diapers: Pay whatever the going rate is for retired diapers—sold by the bag, typically—from your local baby diaper service. These prefold diapers, which are no longer deemed fit in the eyes of the baby diaper service for their clients' high standards, are worth more than their weight in gold for a multitude of applications on a boat. They are ideal for finishing work as well as general cleaning, because they don't leave a bunch of lint in their wake.

Ziploc bags: I call these "poor man's Tupperware"; they are the brightwork artist's primary system of storage, and they keep everything from cut-up sandpaper to foam brushes to masking tape orderly and clean. Keep a box of the 1-quart freezer bags in your materials kit at all times.

bosun's chair: What makes our custom-made Schattauer chair so wonderful: in addition to a rigid plywood seat, there is a side pocket in the shape of a pop can, which holds a varnishing squirt bottle perfectly upright and uncrushed. Frank and Axel Schattauer are two very nice guys carrying on a lovely family business started by their father. Dealing with them is a bonus to having the perfect chair made just for you.

> Schattauer Sails Inc./Frank and Axel Schattauer
> 6010 Seaview Avenue N.W.
> Seattle, Washington 98107
> 206 783 2400
> Fax 206 783 0173
> E-mail tiogaIV@aol.com

safety materials, along with some safety rules for refinishers . . .

3M respirators/masks: 3M makes two types of disposable masks that should be mainstays of any refinisher's arsenal of safety tools.

- #8643: Do not confuse this with a particle mask, the light-weight single-strapped mask made also by 3M. This is the workhorse particulate respirator, which is quilted and double strapped. It is the perfect tight-fitting, thick, disposable mask to don whenever sanding and/or exposing yourself to sawdust of any kind for longer than 30 seconds. It is also often referred to as a dust-mist mask.

- #8247: This is similar to the particulate respirator above, except that it has a charcoal filter layer. This is the mask to wear when working *inside* with varnish and solvent-added oil finishes, to prevent singing by day's end "the solvent-drunk blues."

latex exam gloves: These lightweight and very pliable gloves are available by the box in almost every drugstore in the country. I never varnish or paint without first snapping on a pair. It's ten times easier than cleaning up later with Orange Go-Jo, and the chance of having my hand held at the movies triples for having taken care of them as a matter of course in my finish work.

nitrile gloves: Most rubber gloves will fall apart when exposed to the solvents and grits we use daily in the brightwork trade. These mint green gloves are tenacious and impervious to most solvents, bleaches, and oils. They are manufactured by many companies, and available in myriad weights and sizes.

eye shields: If you don't wear glasses, get into the habit of protecting your eyes whenever working with bleach or any other caustic solution. Many companies make attractive and tinted eye shields; use them when you have a deck to bleach—or risk a trip to the emergency room with a burned cornea (as I once did!).

knee pads: Our backs suffer enough; we have to give our knees a break in advance. Thanks to the skateboard crowd, good strap-on knee pads are easily accessible, and using them religiously makes it possible to spend hours in "brightwork prayer" as we toil away at our sacred work.

the construction rain suit: Don't ruin your skin bleaching without protection, and don't bleach a boat in your expensive foulies. Take a trip to the industrial supply house and pick out a tasteful lemon-yellow construction rain suit. Buy a two-piece suit (jacket and bibs) one size bigger than you think you need (for wearing sweaters underneath in cold weather). And spend the little extra it takes to get one with a bit of a weave in the plastic. It will last longer.

Orange Go-Jo—Goop—3M Paint Buster: These are the products most commonly available for hand cleanup after working with petroleum products. Use them when you forget to wear gloves.

good first-aid kit: Common sense dictates the presence of this kit on every boat and in every shop, and any other place where you expect to conduct the merest sport of life. Augment the traditional collection with a good emergency eye wash, especially if you plan to bleach.

some brightwork safety rules

- Don't be a dope—wear *masks!*—a particulate respirator whenever you sand, and a charcoal-filter mask whenever you varnish indoors.
- Create good cross ventilation—regardless of the temperature—for all interior varnish and oiling work.
- Don't smoke—ever! And absolutely don't let anyone smoke *around* you while you're working with solvents.
- Store all refinishing chemicals in cool places, away from anything you plan to eat or wear.
- "Burp" every can of product that has a solvent base by slowly turning the lid at arm's length to release vapors when opening.
- If you value your senses, cover your eyes, nose, and hands during all work that exposes those parts to toxic materials.
- Do not use solvents to clean paint and varnish from hands; solvents head straight for your liver. If you haven't taken preventive measures to keep hands clean, at least take intelligent steps in removing the mess, by using proper hand cleaning materials.
- Prevent *arrest:* do not pour solvents, varnish, stripper, bleach, or *anything* of a toxic or caustic nature down a storm drain.
- If you hurt yourself badly enough to require more than a big Band-Aid, don't play doctor. Go to the emergency room ASAP.
- Take a proactive look at your work environment, and mitigate in advance any possible disasters. Lower the swim ladder if it's possible to fall overboard as you work; reposition the boom if you have to work underneath it; move mooring lines if they promise to trip you; test all connections with gusto before going aloft in a bosun's chair. In short, *think ahead!*
- Save that beer for the end of the workday; it *isn't* what we're referring to when we specify "brushing liquid . . . "

chapter **13½**

extra! extra!

read all about it!

five books, three cyber sites, and one really corny joke . . .

This book would be incomplete without further reading recommendations. Think of this "half chapter" as homework.

books to love

THE ART OF THE PAINTED FINISH
by Isabel O'Neil

William Morrow & Co. (1971)

Here is a book for the brightwork artist who is crazy about messing around with brushes and varnish and who, once finished transforming a boat, will need other new and exciting canvasses. O'Neil's writing makes me want to go out and transform every wall, piece of furniture, and floor in sight. And with her very thoughtful guidance, I feel sure that whatever I undertake in that mission, I will succeed at joyfully and with inspired patience. In fact, one of my favorite quotes on the patience theme is from this book:

I plead that those who share my admiration, who find beauty in painted surfaces, and who desire the pleasure of rendering them for creative satisfaction, will give themselves a "time for learning." Adults have so little patience with themselves and dogmatically demand an immediate expertise. This is the epitome of arrogance. I have taught so many whose sole equipment was desire that I know excellence can be achieved by anyone similarly embarking on this fascinating journey.

THE WOODBOOK
by Klaus Ulrich Leistikow

Taschen America (2002)

This incredible volume reproduces, in painstaking facsimile, all the specimen pages from the originally published work *American Woods*. That work, 14 volumes with actual specimens culled, assembled, and mounted on card stock by Romeyn Beck Hough between 1888 and 1913, remains an unparalleled publishing achievement, and created a benchmark for study of trees and wood. For each tree, three different cross-section cuts of wood are depicted (radial, horizontal, and vertical) showing the particular characteristics of the grain and the colors and textures to be found among the many different wood species. Also included in this special edition are lithographs by Charles Sprague Sargent of the leaves and nuts of most trees, as well as descriptions of the trees' geographical origins and physical characteristics. This amazing book comes nestled in a plywood box and is a treasure for anyone who appreciates the inherent magic in wood—especially anyone who likes working with wood.

INSTANT WEATHER FORECASTING
by Alan Watts

Dodd, Mead & Company (hard cover) and Sheridan House (paperback), 2nd edition (2001)

This isn't the definitive volume on meteorology; it *is* a succinct guide to reading what we Seattle varnishers have come to regard as *the* standing menace to productivity—*the clouds!* This "clouds bible" delivers more truths about the weather than could be gleaned from two thousand local forecasts. I have played a career-long game of cat and mouse with the workday skies and, thanks to this excellent guide, usually emerged the victor. The heart of the book is the gallery of cloud photographs, each with its own chart delineating the type of weather to follow, including wind, visibility, precipitation, cloud covering, temperature, and atmospheric pressure. For sailors, there is also a wonderful companion volume entitled *Instant Wind Forecasting*.

THE HISTORY OF THE WORLD IN 10½ CHAPTERS
by Julian Barnes

Knopf (hard cover, 1989) and Vintage Books (paperback, 1990)

What's so special about this little work of fiction, and what could it possibly have to do with a book on brightwork?

1. It's one of my all-time favorite books, with an audacious protagonist (a woodworm!) giving a wickedly revisionist account of the sailing of Noah's ark.
2. Its title inspired the one for this book. (Please, Mr. Barnes—see it as flattery and don't call the lawyers.)

Trust me; you'll love this. It is a work of literary—and cynical—genius!

And, amazingly, my publishers don't seem to think it's being too immodest to recommend:

BRIGHTWORK: THE ART OF FINISHING WOOD
by Rebecca J. Wittman

International Marine/McGraw-Hill (1990)

This is a fancy book about brightwork, and the progenitor of the work you currently hold in your hand. It is sometimes accused of being the varnishing bible, but I think people who say that are living dangerously. *Brightwork* has a more narrative style of "how-to" than what you find here, and within that narrative are woven many threads of my own experiences in all aspects of life: family, work, love, loss, failure, success, and travels in the larger arena of humanity. Those threads come together to form a rich contextual tapestry meant to serve as a backdrop for the doing of what can sometimes seem mundane work. The things that you will find in that book that you won't find in this one are not needed in the course of an actual project, and therefore could be set aside in the writing of this one. But in the larger picture they help to provide a deeper understanding of the art, philosophy, and history of the world of varnishing. *Brightwork* was written to help people to learn to think for themselves and ultimately find their own joy in brightwork artistry.

websites to peruse

woodenboat.com

One of the greatest information exchanges to come along in the world of boat building and finishing is the WoodenBoat Online Forum. Log onto this site and you'll have at your fingertips hundreds of archived stream-of-consciousness "chats," ordered and indexed by subject. Typing in the keyword "brightwork" takes you down a labyrinthine path of opinions that can make your head spin!

brightwork.us

(full disclosure: this just happens to be my website . . .)

If you've still got a hankering for scenes from the brightwork universe with Rebecca as your guide, visit this site and discover what's new—along with what never changes!

and . . .

If your work is done and you've got nothing better to entertain you, forget eBay! Visit the following website and take the Varnish Quiz by Bill Rogers:
www.pearsonvanguard.homestead.com/files/varnish_quiz.htm

and finally, a varnish joke

Paula: Hey Debora, I heard your best friend drowned in a tub of varnish. How awful!

Debora: Yeah. But what a finish!

index

sanding finishes, 60
sanding teak decks, 121
varnishing, 93
toxic waste disposal, 53, 57, 59, 165
trisodium phosphate (TSP), for deck
cleaning, 114, 149
tung oil
for interior oil finish, 88–91
in linseed oil sealer, 82, 83
as prevarnish sealer, 81, 91
recommended brand, 153
removing from fiberglass, 73, 99,
161
in varnish, 32
turpentine, 160

U
UV package, in varnish, 32, 126

V
vacuum cleaner, 51, 53, 58, 59, 60,
61, 93, 110–11, 120, 121,
122–23, 139
varnish
components of, 31–32
history, 16
protective qualities, 23
recommended brands, 111,
158–59
removing from fiberglass, 73, 99
shelf life, 32
stirring, 94, 158
thinning, 33–34, 94, 97, 159
tips for handling, 158
water-based, 159
as wood sealer, 81–82

varnish finish
application of, 93–99
assessing deterioration of, 24, 103
maintenance and repair, 24–25,
101–5
varnishing
cabin soles, 110–11
cleanup, 73, 99
coatings schedule, 96–97
materials and equipment, 93, 94,
156–59
preliminary cleaning, 94
procedure for large areas, 95, 106,
126
refresher coats, 24, 101–2
spars, 124–34
taping, 94, 96
tips for, 95–96
tool bag, 138
weather factors, 95–96, 97, 98
varnishing window, 98
varnish quiz, 170
varnish thinners. *See also* solvents
for sealer coats, 81–82
wise use of, 33–34, 97, 159
veneer. *See also* cabin soles
finish required on, 23
sanding precautions, 66, 89

W
water-based varnishes, 159
water stains, removing, 67–69, 149
weather
for acid bleaching, 46
for applying sealer, 82
for applying stains, 78

for bleaching stains, 67
for chemical stripping, 55
for dry-scraping, 58
for heat stripping, 51
organizing according to, 40, 95–96
planning projects by season, 39,
112
for sanding finishes, 60
for sanding teak decks, 121
for spar varnishing, 134
varnish drying times and, 33,
81–82, 97
for varnishing, 93
weather forecasting aids, 40
Web addresses. *See* Internet
resources
wet-or-dry sandpaper, 84, 88, 150
wet-sanded oil sealer, 81, 91
The Woodbook (Leistikow), 167–68
Woodcraft Supply Co., 54
wood fillers, paste, 77, 81, 91

Z
Ziploc bags, 42, 74, 93, 121, 122,
131, 133, 138, 162–63

photo credits

The author and publisher would like to thank the following for their photographs. The page numbers on which their photos are found appear after their names:

Neil Rabinowitz: 2, 9, 10, 11, 12, 34, 38, 44, 53, 62, 63, 75, 76, 77, 80, 83, 84, 86, 92, 100, 166, 170

Benjamin Mendlowitz: 1, 5, 19, 20, 35, 36, 42, 48, 71, 98

Billy Black: 26, 30, 160

Greg L'Esperance: 14

All other photos are by the author.